Children with Disabilities:
Reading and Writing the Four-Blocks® Way

by
Karen A. Erickson and
David A. Koppenhaver

Carson-Dellosa Publishing Company, Inc.
Greensboro, North Carolina

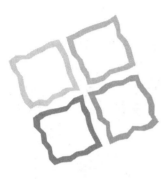

Credits

Editor: Joey Bland

Layout Design: Lori Jackson

Inside Illustrations: Robin Bauer

Cover Design: Matthew Van Zomeren

Cover Illustrations: Matthew Van Zomeren

Printed in the USA • All rights reserved.   ISBN 978-1-60022-125-5

Table of Contents

Children with Disabilities: Reading and Writing the Four-Blocks® Way • CD-104235 • © Carson-Dellosa

Table of Contents

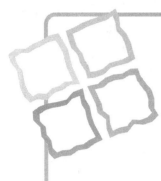

Why Did We Write This Book?

The Four-Blocks® Literacy Framework was initially created in 1989 in an attempt to develop daily instruction that responded to individual differences in classrooms (Cunningham, Hall, and Defee, 1991). The Four Blocks—Guided Reading, Self-Selected Reading, Writing, and Working with Words—represent four different approaches to teaching children to read. The Four-Blocks® Framework acknowledges that children do not all learn in the same way. Consequently, the framework provides them with a range of experiences to support various learning preferences and profiles of relative strengths and weaknesses. Four Blocks also acknowledges that children differ in their literacy competence and consequently attempts to make each Block as multilevel as possible (Cunningham, Hall, and Sigmon, 1999).

We first learned about Four Blocks in the early 1990s from Jim Cunningham, our professor at the University of North Carolina at Chapel Hill. Through our collaboration at the Center for Literacy and Disability Studies, we have used the Four-Blocks® Framework to help children with a broad range of disabilities learn to read and write. We have used Four Blocks to help children with severe cognitive impairments improve their ability to read with understanding. We have used Four Blocks to help children with learning disabilities learn to decode and apply those skills in real reading and writing. We have used Four Blocks to help children who could not talk improve their ability to converse with peers and teachers through improved spelling and writing. We have even used Four Blocks to support an entire field of assistive technology service providers and manufacturers in developing a comprehensive view of effective literacy instruction.

As calls for systematic instruction have increased in recent years, we have held firmly to the Four-Blocks® Framework as an example of research-based, systematic instruction that addresses literacy instruction in a comprehensive manner. We have found that the Four-Blocks® Framework can address the type of systematic phonics instruction many children with disabilities require without neglecting the need to support their continued development of fluency, comprehension, and motivation to read and write. Our experience and research with students with a broad range of disabilities have left us convinced that there is no single program that will address all of their literacy learning needs, nor is there a single program that will address any individual child's needs over time. While there is no simple answer to the reading difficulties experienced by children with disabilities in our schools, the Four-Blocks® Framework provides an organizing structure for the complex answers.

We have written this book first and foremost to support the efforts of general education teachers and the children they teach with disabilities in their inclusive classrooms. We have learned firsthand that children with disabilities require significant supports and informed teachers to succeed in any instructional

Children with Disabilities: Reading and Writing the Four-Blocks® Way • CD-104235 • © Carson-Dellosa

setting. We believe that the Four-Blocks® Framework provides that significant support. We hope the ideas, strategies, and resources shared in this text will contribute to informing teachers of ways to truly meet the learning needs and preferences of **all** students in the general classroom.

In writing this book, we also hope to help teachers working in special education classrooms have more success in teaching their students to read and write so that these students might gain greater and more successful access to the general education program. While we believe the social, linguistic, and cultural contexts of general education classrooms create richer and more varied supports for literacy learning, the principles of instruction in the Four-Blocks® Framework apply equally to children in general education or special education environments. The critical issue is how to make good instruction accessible given the nature of children's significant differences in areas such as understanding what a teacher says, accessing writing tools, seeing texts, or attending to lessons.

Individual Differences That Impact Literacy Learning

In order to make the Four-Blocks® Framework accessible to children with disabilities, we consider six general areas where children with disabilities often differ in significant ways from their classmates. These differences are significant because they impact the relative success or difficulty that children experience while participating in literacy activities. The six areas include **communication**, **cognition**, **physical abilities**, **senses** (primarily vision and hearing), **affect**, and **attention**. As educators, we find that these areas of potential difference are more informative to instructional planning than the label assigned to characterize a student's type of disability (health impairment, learning disability, etc.).

For example, if a teacher is told that Edgar is going to be in her second-grade class and that Edgar has autism, she is unsure of what, if anything, she must modify to help Edgar learn to read and write. If, however, the teacher reads in Edgar's student file that he can respond successfully to direct questions and requests, but he has difficulty initiating conversations or asking his own questions (i.e., he has significant communication differences), then the teacher can structure Guided Reading lessons to support his successful participation. If a teacher learns that Edgar can attend closely and for long periods of time to computer-supported activities but that he has difficulty engaging in paper-and-pencil tasks (i.e., significant attention differences), then she can incorporate technologies to support Edgar's writing. If the teacher observes that Edgar is successful participating and learning in small groups but that he is frustrated by working independently (i.e., significant affective differences), then the teacher can use Edgar's peers to support his engagement in Self-Selected Reading.

Once we have identified one or more significant differences, our problem-solving efforts focus on identifying or developing adaptations that neither change the fundamental nature of an activity nor make it more difficult or less desirable for children to achieve than the original activity. For example, the Word Wall is a central component of the Working with Words Block. The purposes of the Word Wall are to teach children to read and spell words with automaticity and accuracy, while teaching them strategies to use the known words on the wall to read and spell unknown words. (For a more complete description, see pages 123–124 in *The Teacher's*

Why Did We Write This Book?

Guide to the Four Blocks® by Cunningham, Hall, and Sigmon, Carson-Dellosa, 1999.) One possible modification for a Word Wall might be to provide children with a portable chart that has each of the words written on a card and attached with hook-and-loop tape. Such a modification might serve several purposes such as:

- increasing the child's attention by providing materials to manipulate

- increasing the child's ability to indicate if she cannot speak

- increasing the child's ability to see the words if she has low vision

- increasing the child's success in selecting the correct words for the activities that involve the Word Wall

During a Word Wall lesson, this modification would allow children to participate by selecting whole words that the teacher has asked the class to identify or write. This particular modification should **not** enable children to participate without ever spelling the words letter by letter. If this were the only modification provided, children would be less likely to develop automaticity and accuracy in spelling or to use knowledge of those words to read and spell other words. However, providing children not only with whole words to use in identifying and talking about the Word Wall but also with individual letters to use in spelling the words would enable them to engage in the same spelling practice as the rest of the class. The instructional goal of the original activity would be maintained while access to the activity has been modified.

Children may have significant differences in one or more of the six areas that require adaptations of the materials, instruction, or environment. These differences may be mild as in the case of children who have partial hearing loss in one ear. These differences may be moderate as in the case of children with Down syndrome who struggle with conceptual learning, such as responding to **wh-** questions. These differences may be severe as in the case of girls with Rett syndrome who have limited or no use of their hands and little or no speech.

Some teachers may find it difficult to plan and implement literacy instruction for children with significant communication impairments. These teachers may find it difficult to imagine how children who cannot talk can learn to read and write, or they may be unsure of how to interact with children who point to pictures in lieu of talking. Other teachers may find it difficult to plan and implement literacy instruction for children with multiple disabilities (i.e., those students who may have severe communication, cognitive, **and** physical impairments). These teachers may find it difficult, for example, to support writing when children cannot spell, hold a pencil, or convey in speech their interests or experiences. It is our intent in this book to suggest specific adaptations, strategies, and resources to support the learning of these and other children with disabilities.

A Technology Primer

We wrote this book for one final reason: to increase teachers' awareness and use of the wide variety of technologies that now make it possible for children with disabilities not just to participate in, but, more importantly, to succeed in the general education reading and writing

Why Did We Write This Book?

curriculum. Technologies can increase children's productivity, simplify complex tasks, provide informative feedback, supply a voice for children who cannot speak, replace pencils and books for children whose fingers or hands cannot manipulate traditional tools and media, and meet a variety of sensory needs. We hope that readers will view these technologies as tools (i.e., as means to ends). Technology **does not** replace good instruction; it makes good instruction more accessible given the nature of children's significant differences. When we consider the use of technology in the classroom and beyond, we constantly remind ourselves that technology involves both method and material. Its value is determined by children's increased participation, understanding, and feelings of competence, not to mention classmates' and teachers' greater awareness of these students' capabilities and feelings.

This initial discussion of technology is intended to provide a few examples of the types of technologies we will address in this book. It is also intended to highlight some of the rules and problem-solving strategies that we employ in making decisions regarding the types of technological supports we provide children with special needs engaged in literacy learning and use.

Technology in special education is called "assistive technology" because it serves a supportive role. Within the category of assistive technology, there are both light-tech and high-tech methods and materials that support children in accessing classroom instruction. Light-tech involves tools that are not computer based, such as a headstick pointer for children with cerebral palsy who cannot use their fingers. High-tech includes computer-based tools, such as software that enables children with significant health impairments, who may not be able to hold a pencil or who fatigue rapidly, to dictate text into a word processor or control a computer with voice commands. Assistive technologies extend well beyond classroom use and include such items as wheelchairs and leg braces. We will limit our discussions in this book to instructional applications of assistive technologies that support participation and learning in literacy experiences.

Many of the light-tech suggestions in this book require little more than a new way to use many of the materials already in classrooms, schools, and homes. On the other hand, some of the high-tech suggestions extend well beyond the scope of the computers that line the back wall of the classroom or the computer lab down the hall. While we will attempt to provide examples for uses of existing technologies, such as word processing and drawing programs, we will also attempt to highlight new technologies that may support particular children.

High-tech solutions for reading and writing can be described in terms of the level of support they provide children. For example, one common solution to significant differences in hand use is a word processing program on a standard computer. We often see computers with word processors listed as modifications on Individualized Education Programs (IEPs). Children who need modifications to meet physical needs often achieve dramatic improvements in the quantity and quality of their writing when schools support them in using a word processing program and standard computer keyboard rather than a pen or pencil.

Why Did We Write This Book?

Children with severe or multiple impairments, however, often require more than a word processing program. For example, sometimes a talking word processor provides additional support that children with attention or mild cognitive impairments require. Hearing the computer say letters as they are typed, pronounce whole words when a space is typed after a string of letters, or read whole sentences when end punctuation is typed provides the feedback they require to remain focused on the writing task at hand.

Sometimes children's physical limitations are so severe that an alternative to the regular keyboard or typing is required. Alternative keyboards have much larger keys and are flexible in terms of key arrangement (for example, frequency order instead of QWERTY) and content (for example, pictures or words or phrases instead of letters). Touching a picture key can result in a whole word or phrase being typed into the word processing program (talking or not).

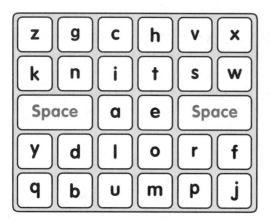

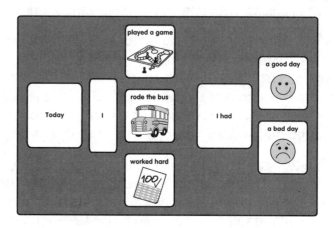

Alternative keyboards can also support children with visual impairments because textured symbols or Braille can be used on the keyboard layout.

Sometimes children's physical impairments, language impairments, or spelling difficulties are so severe that word prediction software is required. Word prediction software is used in combination with a child's word processor. As the child types the first letter of a word, the prediction software

Children with Disabilities: Reading and Writing the Four-Blocks® Way • CD-104235 • © Carson-Dellosa

shows a list of words it predicts the child is trying to type. This prediction is based on the child's written vocabulary, words the child has typed most recently, frequency of words in the English language, and rules of grammar. If the word that the child is trying to type is in the list, the child can select the word with a second keystroke. If the child is unable to read the words, she can point to each with the cursor and hear the computer speak the words aloud.

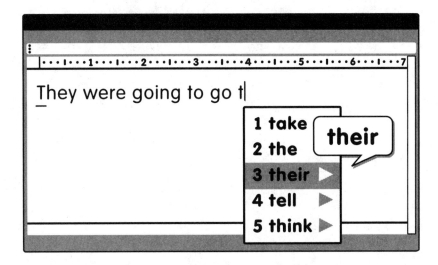

Sometimes children's cognitive or learning impairments are so severe that planning software is required. Planning software is typically used with a teacher or another adult's assistance for children in grades 1–3. Planning software allows children to generate ideas they want to write about. The software enables brainstorming, connecting of ideas, or sequencing of information. Picture and graphic support can be added to the resulting computer-based web. Planning software also will transform a web into a sequential outline that can be pasted into a word processor to guide the child's writing.

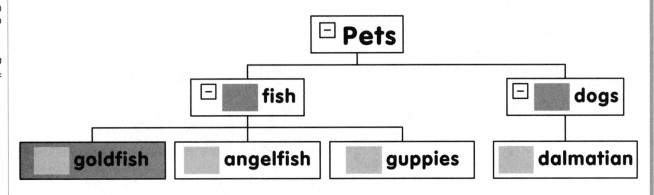

Why Did We Write This Book?

Some children's communication impairments are so severe that they cannot speak intelligibly or they cannot speak at all. These children often require augmentative and alternative communication (AAC) devices that provide a means to converse with others. Communication software   and hardware provides such children with the tools that they require to interact with classmates and adults. Typically, communication devices enable children to select pictures, letters, or words and combine them into messages that are spoken by the device using synthesized or digitized speech. Many of these devices can also be attached to computers to become alternative keyboards and allow the child to use the same device both for spoken and for written communication. There are also communication software programs that can be loaded into a computer, typically a laptop, that can accompany children in different environments.

Good sources for additional information about technologies for supporting children with disabilities may be found on the Internet. Linda Burkhart's Web site (*http://www.lburkhart.com/*) includes ideas for adapting instructional materials, using the Internet in classrooms, and teaching in single-computer classrooms and links to other useful resources. The Web site of the National Center to Improve Practice (*http://www2.edc.org/NCIP*) has information about classroom technology as well as video clips of children with disabilities using these technologies to participate in both general education and special education classrooms. Finally, Special Education Training British Columbia (*http://www.setbc.org*) has information specifically about technologies that support the implementation of the Four-Blocks with students with sensory or communication impairments.

The Assistive Technology Industry Association (ATIA) is a not-for-profit membership organization of manufacturers, sellers, or providers of technology-based assistive devices and/or services. Their members include those who are focused on a variety of assistive technologies including augmentative and alternative communication (AAC) devices. ATIA hosts an annual conference and their Web site offers links to all of its members' Web sites. For more information go to http://www.atia.org.

To reiterate, we see this book as a companion text to *The Teacher's Guide to the Four Blocks®* (Cunningham, Hall, and Sigmon, 1999). We have used Four Blocks long enough with sufficient success to believe that good instruction is good instruction. We do not believe that a different curriculum is required in order for children with disabilities to succeed in learning to read and write. We have learned, however, that teachers must attend consciously and thoughtfully to the significant learning differences of children with disabilities in order to make good instruction accessible to these students. We hope that this book will help teachers accomplish the goal of teaching **all** children to read and write.

Why Did We Write This Book?

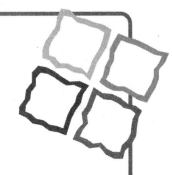

Overview

The remaining chapters of this book largely parallel those of *The Teacher's Guide to the Four Blocks*® (Cunningham, Hall, and Sigmon, 1999). We have not attempted to explain the Blocks in detail. The original authors did that wonderfully. What we have attempted is a succinct explanation of the impact of individual differences on learning opportunity and access to the materials and experiences central to each Block. We describe adaptations and modifications of tools, materials, experiences, and the classroom that we have developed or observed other teachers use in teaching children with disabilities to read and write. Following are two descriptions of a day in a Four-Blocks primary classroom. The first is a look at the same classroom described on pages 4–19 in *The Teacher's Guide to the Four Blocks*® but with the addition of children with disabilities. The second description is that of a special education classroom implementing the Four Blocks. While we include a schedule with activities, such as snack and physical education, so that teachers may have a clear view of the flow of the day, we describe in detail only the literacy instruction.

Sample Four-Blocks Day in an Inclusive Classroom

Children with disabilities have special needs that may require significant support of special educators and related services personnel, such as speech-language pathologists (SLPs), if they are to succeed in general education. They require instructional adaptations and the integrated use of technologies. They push the concepts of multimethod and multilevel beyond the current comfort level of many of us as classroom teachers.

This inclusive classroom has three children with special needs. The first is a boy, James. James has an educational label of language and learning disabilities. What is important to know about James is that he has difficulty following multistep verbal directions. He can attend for long periods of time when he is in interactive settings, if he has the supports of visual models and step-by-step verbal directions. He enjoys social interactions with his peers. He is very much aware of the differences between his reading and writing skills and those of his peers.

The second child is a girl, Linda. She has a medical diagnosis of Down syndrome and an educational label of mental retardation. It is important to know that Linda is highly motivated to pursue her own broad interests. She is very social and enjoys being with other children at all times. Given opportunity, she attempts to take a leadership role in play and academic pursuits—even if she doesn't quite understand the activity. Her speech is difficult to understand and is limited to three- and four-word phrases, but her peers seem to have little difficulty in communicating effectively with her. Fine motor impairments make it difficult for her to write with a pen or pencil; nonetheless, she prefers them to the computer. Linda loves books.

Children with Disabilities: Reading and Writing the Four-Blocks® Way • CD-104235 • © Carson-Dellosa

Overview: Sample Day

The third child is Alyssa. Alyssa has a medical diagnosis of spastic cerebral palsy and an educational label of multiple impairments. Alyssa's body language suggests that she enjoys being in school. She can communicate via facial expressions and is learning to use her eyes to look at choices presented approximately two feet in front of her on a clear acrylic board called an eye-gaze frame. It is unclear what her cognitive level is because she has no clear way to demonstrate what she does and does not know. Her physical impairments are such that she is unable to use her hands purposefully.

One of the key tenets of inclusion is that the proportion of children with disabilities in any given class should match the natural proportions of people with disabilities in the community. Clustering children with disabilities in classrooms designated as "inclusion" classes is often viewed as a more efficient means of including children with disabilities in order to pool resources and support services. Unfortunately, having more than one child with significant disabilities or a few children with mild or moderate disabilities can stretch teachers and general education resources to frustrating limits. Nonetheless, for the purpose of describing how children with a range of disabilities can be included in mainstream Four-Blocks classrooms, James, Linda, and Alyssa are all members of this classroom.

Opening (10–20 minutes)

10–20 minutes

The children enter and prepare for the day. One of Linda's friends has walked with her from the bus and reminds her that the teacher is waiting for them on the rug. Linda and her friend sit down as the children begin to share the activities that they enjoyed over the weekend. A teaching assistant gets Alyssa's BIGmack® (AbleNet, Inc.) out of her backpack and puts it on her wheelchair tray. Before another child has finished talking, Alyssa puts her hand on the four-inch round BIGmack® producing the recorded message, "I got to go to the mall this weekend." The teacher reminds Alyssa to wait for others to finish before she shares.

She also reminds the teaching assistant to leave the BIGmack® on the wheelchair tray to help Alyssa learn to listen and wait rather than responding reflexively and touching the BIGmack® whenever it is placed on her tray. When the first child finishes, the teacher returns to Alyssa, "What were you telling us about your weekend, Alyssa?" It takes a few seconds, but Alyssa touches the BIGmack® again. Other children chime in with their own family adventures.

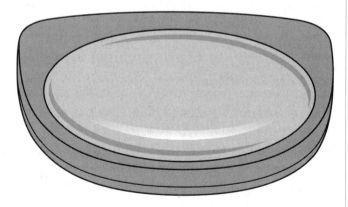

Children with Disabilities: Reading and Writing the Four-Blocks® Way • CD-104235 • © Carson-Dellosa

Overview: Sample Day

Then, the teacher shows the children several new books about animals that she is going to place in a book basket. One child asks, "Does that mean we're gonna learn about animals?" The teacher responds, "You're right! Whenever we start a new unit in social studies or science, I gather new library books." All of the children are anxious to look at the books, but it is the teacher's policy that they have to wait until Self-Selected Reading time. She has found that this practice heightens children's interest. However, she quickly learned this year that what enticed other children merely frustrated Linda. In the first week of school, Linda missed Guided Reading twice when her insistence on looking at the books escalated into emotional outbursts that required her temporary removal from the classroom. Rather than give in to Linda's demands or continue to remove her from instruction she needed, the team devised a plan to allow Linda to explore the books for a few minutes until a timer signaled a transition to Guided Reading. Now three weeks later, Linda needs only a verbal reminder that she can look at the book for just a few minutes until Guided Reading begins. Over the next few weeks, the team will work with Linda to select the book she will look at later and put it in a special spot. The team is confident that before the end of the year, Linda will be able to wait just like all of the other children.

30–40 minutes

The Guided Reading Block (30–40 minutes)

This morning, the teacher has selected *Spiders* by Gail Gibbons (Holiday House, 1994) for the Guided Reading lesson. The book relates to their new unit on animals and is at the average reading level of her class. The class will read this book for three days this week and will read an easier book on Thursday and Friday. The school has 15 copies of *Spiders*, which the teacher has checked out.

With the help of the occupational therapist (OT) and the SLP who work with Alyssa, the teacher has also created an adapted version of the book for the computer. The OT scanned and imported the illustrations into a multimedia software program. She also added a few mpeg videos of spiders to augment Alyssa's understanding by searching the Internet with the AltaVista video search engine (*http://www.altavista. com/video/default*). The SLP added the text, which the computer will read aloud in synthesized speech when the volume is turned up. Clicking the mouse can turn the pages of the resulting electronic book. The mouse has been put into a small cardboard box that has been turned into a "mouse house" so that Alyssa will not push the mouse away accidentally and instead can turn the pages independently by hitting the top of the box.

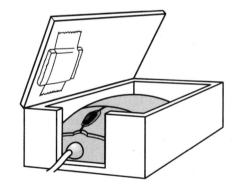

Overview: Sample Day

When the special education team first suggested adding these electronic, adapted versions of the books to the school's multiple-copy library, the librarian raised concerns about copyright law. The OT's research revealed that books can be adapted to be accessible for individual children with special needs as long as the adaptations are not reproduced or distributed separately from the original version. The multiple-copy library now stores one adapted copy of each title on a read-only CD inside a plastic pocket on the back cover of the book. The electronic version can only be used with the disk inserted, and the original version of the book is placed right next to the computer, often in the hands of a reading partner, when the CD is in use.

Before the children arrived this morning, the teacher marked a good stopping point in the books with paper clips and index cards. She put the same reminder on a sticky note attached to the computer screen where Alyssa will read with her partner. The teacher carefully assigns partners to work with Alyssa and the other children with special needs in the class. Her goal is to create pairs that can work together productively and independently. The first pair she calls always includes Alyssa because it takes a few minutes to load the electronic version of the book. As she calls each remaining pair to the reading area, she hands them a copy of the book and tells them that they may look at the book while they are waiting but that they cannot remove or go past the paper clip. She gives Linda's partner a reminder to make sure she gives Linda a chance to talk about the illustrations, and she gives James's partner a reminder to give him enough time before helping with difficult words. The entire routine is familiar to everyone since the teacher often uses a paper clip to show students where to stop and encourages them to look at the illustrations while they wait for everyone to gather.

Once the class has assembled, the teacher notes how comfortable she has become with the mixture of children sitting in chairs and on the rug during Guided Reading. She recalls the first few weeks of school when she and the aide tried to take Alyssa out of her chair to sit on the floor with her peers so that everyone was physically equal. Putting her back in her chair and getting set to read took almost all of the time they had allotted for partner reading. The teacher remembers what a difficult time James and Linda had sitting in undefined spaces on the floor with their peers all around. She remembers that first difficult conversation with the special education teacher, when she wondered how she would ever manage with such difficult children in her already busy room.

Now, the solution seems so simple. Some children can sit better and attend more easily when they are in chairs. Others do better on the floor. Alyssa is now sitting next to a peer in the "chair row." James sits in a child-size rocking chair that allows him to move without disturbing his peers. Linda, motivated to sit with her friends who were in the "floor row," has learned to use a carpet square to help her remain in her personal space.

Children with Disabilities: Reading and Writing the Four-Blocks® Way • CD-104235 • © Carson-Dellosa

Overview: Sample Day

Picture Walk

The teacher introduces the new book with a "picture walk." She asks everyone to look at the book cover in order to identify the title and author. After students discuss the cover, they continue exploring the remaining pages up to the paper clip. They name all of the things they see and read captions and labels together with the teacher. The teacher highlights phonetic spellings, like **uh-RACK-nid**, pronouncing them herself and asking children to pronounce them with her. After they have read three words together, she says, "Okay, everyone, let's read them once more. This time, let's read them in our heads like Alyssa does. Ready?" Then, she points to each part and hums each syllable as she points to it. Before Alyssa came to her class, the teacher knew that readers have inner voices that they use when they read, but she had never considered teaching children about their inner voices. Recently, she has noticed that her class is quieter during Self-Selected Reading. It seems that more children are developing their ability to read silently. She wonders how much her efforts to make Alyssa aware of her inner voice have influenced the development of this skill in all of the children.

The teacher reminds the class to write a few facts they learn about spiders on their index cards when they finish the assigned reading. Alyssa's partner knows that she and Alyssa will each pick a fact from a list that the teacher has written on a sheet of paper next to the computer. Since Alyssa doesn't have any way to talk about or write what she learned, the teacher has prepared a list of five facts about spiders from the book. All of the facts are in the book, but only three appear in the section the children are reading for today. After Alyssa and her partner finish reading, the partner will read each fact aloud and ask Alyssa if that is the one she wants to share with the group. Next she will record the fact on the BIGmack® (AbleNet, Inc.) for Alyssa to share with the group when they reconvene. Finally, the partner will select her own fact to share.

Partner Reading

The timer is set for 12 minutes of partner reading. Children spread out around the room. James and his partner would like to sit on the pillows in the reading area, but the teacher reminds them how difficult it is for them to remain on task when they are not sitting in chairs. They compromise and sit together in the teacher's big rocking chair. James holds the book, turns the pages, and describes the pictures while his partner does all of the reading.

Linda and her partner are sitting next to each other with their backs against the wall. Linda points to the title and reads, "Spiders," before turning the page, pointing to the title again, and reading "Spiders." Linda's partner, Katie, has figured out various ways to get Linda involved in the reading. Today, Katie stops when she comes to the word **spider** while reading, points, and says, "You read it, Linda." Linda eagerly examines the word and says, "spider," on each occasion.

Overview: Sample Day

Alyssa and her partner sit at the computer. Alyssa is hitting the top of the mouse house with her hand to "turn the page" each time her partner pauses at the end of a page of text. The instructional assistant turned off the sound before she left Alyssa and her partner at the computer to finish their reading for the day. Later, during Self-Selected Reading, Alyssa can chose to reread this section of her book with the sound turned on.

As the teacher circulates, she listens to partners read and compliments them on both their reading and their cooperation. She reminds James and Alyssa that they are listening to their partners read, so that they can share one new thing they have learned about spiders with the whole group.

After 12 minutes, the timer sounds, and the children move back to the reading area. Pairs who have not finished reading gather also and finish their reading while the teacher moves on with the lesson. While a couple of children continue to read, the teacher starts recording the spider facts that children share. She tries to include James and Linda early in the sharing process so that they can successfully share a new fact they learned. She often explicitly asks Alyssa for a contribution if Alyssa doesn't contribute independently with her BIGmack® (AbleNet, Inc.). Once all of the children have had a chance to share new spider facts, the teacher collects the books and reminds the children that they will finish reading the book and adding more facts to their chart tomorrow.

The Working with Words Block (30 minutes)

Following the Guided Reading Block, the children go to their seats and get ready for the Working with Words Block. Every day, the children complete a Word Wall activity and another activity that is designed to develop decoding and spelling skills. Linda goes to the computer that Alyssa had been using and independently launches the word processing program she will need. Using the computer keyboard during the first portion of the Working with Words Block allows Linda to keep up with the pace of the lesson since her handwriting is so labored.

30 minutes

Word Walls

Each Monday, the teacher adds five new words to the Word Wall. The five words are carefully selected to represent words that children need for their reading and writing. The words are arranged alphabetically by first letter and have colorful paper behind them to help children attend to the shapes of the words. This year, the words on the wall all have fluorescent colors behind them, and the teacher has had to be more careful than in the past in planning what color goes with each word. Instead of simply making sure that similar words were different colors, the teacher has to make sure that each of seven colors is used with each initial letter before any of the seven is repeated.

Children with Disabilities: Reading and Writing the Four-Blocks® Way • CD-104235 • © Carson-Dellosa

Overview: Sample Day

The color-coding has taken on a new significance this year because of Alyssa, James, and Linda. Alyssa uses a clear acrylic eye-gaze frame during the Word Wall lessons. When the speech-language pathologist first tried to explain the system to the teacher, she could not imagine how Alyssa was going to use it. The system allows Alyssa to look at one of seven locations on a piece of 24" x 24" (60.96 cm x 60.96 cm) clear acrylic mounted vertically at the end of her wheelchair tray in order to communicate with an adult facing her on the other side.

During a Word Wall lesson, Alyssa can indicate what letter the word starts with by looking at the block of letters that contains the first letter and then indicating the specific letter with a second look that communicates the relative location of the letter (upper/lower, middle, left, right) or color of the letter. Once the adult has confirmed the letter, Alyssa indicates the color of the word by looking at the colorful block that matches the word on the Word Wall.

When the children clap, chant, and write the words, Alyssa uses the same encoding system to first identify the group in which the letter appears and then indicating the relative location or color. Alyssa's goal is really to learn letter names and sounds. Participation in the Working with Words Block gives her multiple, meaningful opportunities to work on those skills every day.

James and Linda have also played a role in the teacher's more thoughtful approach to the use of colors. She selected fluorescent paper for the Word Wall this year because it would make it easier for her to create portable, color-coded Word Walls for James and Linda. Each Monday morning, the two students give their Word Wall folders to the teacher. She adds the five new words for the week using a permanent black marker outlining the shape of each. Then, she color-codes the word using a highlighter that corresponds to the color she used on the classroom Word Wall example.

Adding New Words
The teacher adds the five new words to the classroom Word Wall as the children watch her. She underlines the spelling pattern and attaches gold stars to the words that will be helpful to the children in reading and spelling other words. (She has marked gold stars with a pen in the

portable Word Walls, as well.) She reminds the children that she has selected these five words because they are words they see often in books and need when they write.

Because it is Monday, the teacher asks children to clap, chant, and write the five new words she has just added to the wall. For the first few days of the week, they practice the new words, but toward the end of the week, they will also practice words that were added earlier in the year. Today, as on all Mondays, the teacher gives clues that help the children focus on the spelling of the words. "The word I want you to practice is our new **wh-** word. Who can tell me what it is?" The children know to look for the word, raise their hands when they find it, and say it in their heads while James and Linda have a chance to find the words on their portable Word Walls and Alyssa has a chance to tell the adult working with her which color the new word is.

When the teacher sees Alyssa look at her, she asks everyone to say the new word together. They respond, "Where." The teacher then points out **where** on the Word Wall as she walks by Linda and James to make sure that they have their fingers on the correct word on their portable Word Walls. She then leads the children as they clap rhythmically and chant the letters three times: "**w-h-e-r-e, w-h-e-r-e, w-h-e-r-e—where**!" After they have chanted aloud, she leads them in their silent chant. As she watches the children nod their head emphatically at exactly the moment they should say the final **where** in their silent chants, she smiles to herself, realizing yet another way that Alyssa has added to their word-learning success. Finally, all of the children write the word as Linda types it on the computer and Alyssa works to tell the assistant what the first letter is. The entire class repeats the cycle for the remaining four words that were added to the wall today.

Making Words
As the children move into the second Working with Words activity, the printer finishes printing Linda's work, and she moves to her seat at the table with her peers. Today the children are doing a Making Words activity. Each child is given five consonants printed in black on laminated pieces of card stock (for example, **b,b,g,n,s**) and two vowels printed in red on similar cards (for example, **i, o**). The instructional assistant who will be working with Alyssa uses restickable note tape to hang the letters on a clear acrylic frame. She also puts a symbol on Alyssa's tray that indicates, "That's not the one I want." Alyssa will look at the letters she wants in the order that she wants them. She will use the symbol on her tray to communicate when she has made a mistake and wants to redo something. At this point Alyssa is using all uppercase letters for this and other word study activities. When she begins spelling words and writing texts, the team will find an accommodation that will allow her to easily handle both uppercase and lowercase letters. For now, the visual distinctiveness of uppercase letters make them the most appropriate choice.

Children with Disabilities: Reading and Writing the Four-Blocks® Way • CD-104235 • © Carson-Dellosa

Overview: Sample Day

While children are getting the appropriate letter cards, the teacher is putting a matching set of larger cards into a pocket chart at the front of the classroom. Then, she asks children to check that the letter cards they have match the cards in the pocket chart. Once all children are sure that they have the same vowels and consonants as the teacher, the teacher begins the lesson. She writes a **2** on the board and tells students they will start by making the two-letter word, **in**.

She circulates through the room while children make the word. She is careful to watch the children whom she knows are likely to have success only with the first few words and calls on them to make the two- and three-letter words in the pocket chart at the front of the room as often as possible. Today, Linda has been successful and proudly goes up front to make the word in the chart. She also puts the index card with the word **in** written on it in the pocket chart. Later in the lesson, both Linda and James will get copies of the index card put on their desks to help them self-correct and better keep pace with the lesson. Earlier in the year, the teacher tried to slow the pace to meet the needs of these two students in particular and found that she was not keeping the attention of other students. She tried pacing the lesson more quickly, trying not to worry that Linda and James were not making all of the words, but soon discovered that the two grew increasingly frustrated. Creating two additional sets of index cards for each lesson provided a workable alternative. A parent volunteer was happy to write out the cards over a weekend, and, since Linda and James sit at adjacent tables, the teacher quickly adapted to putting cards on their desks as soon as they had finished each of the longer words.

For many children with physical impairments, the added keystrokes and communication exchanges required to use uppercase and lowercase letters when writing dramatically increases the physical demands of writing. In this case, children could write using all caps. When ending punctuation is used, most word processing programs can automatically correct the case. For example, in Microsoft Word® the entire sample can be selected (Edit – Select All; control + A), and the case can be changed to sentence case (Format – Change Case – Sentence Case).

Alyssa is a different story. She cannot keep up with the pace of the lesson and does not appear to have sufficient literacy skills at present to spell words. The team had numerous discussions about the most appropriate way to include Alyssa in the lesson. For now, Alyssa works on making the one- and two-letter words in the same way as her peers at the beginning of the lesson. As the words get longer, the focus shifts to identifying the first letter of each of the words. When the rest of the class moves on to word sorts and transfer activities, so does Alyssa.

The word sort and transfer portion of the Making Words lessons requires little modification for the three children with special needs. Linda and James often volunteer to sort the words, and the teacher is encouraged by the fact that both have begun to look beyond first-letter

Children with Disabilities: Reading and Writing the Four-Blocks® Way • CD-104235 • © Carson-Dellosa

O v e r v i e w :   S a m p l e   D a y

similarities in the sorts. Since it is nearly impossible to interpret which letter Alyssa is pointing to with her eye gaze when she has more than seven or eight choices, it is difficult for her to sort; furthermore, she has no means by which to indicate the trait she used in her sorting scheme. She is, however, able to select from a subset of the words and indicate which words share a characteristic with a set that someone else has begun. She also participates in the transfer portion of the lesson. She consistently indicates which words share similar spelling patterns to the transfer word by looking at her choice from the two that the teaching assistant holds up and reads for her. The team suspects that Alyssa is using rhyming as her primary strategy in completing the transfer step.

Homework Sheet

As she has always done, the teacher prepares Making Words homework sheets for every lesson she completes. The children take the sheets home, cut off the letters, make as many words as they can, and record those words in boxes. The homework sheets have been modified slightly for Linda and James since they have difficulty generating more than one or two words independently. They go home with a list of words written on a separate sheet, and their parents guide them through making as many of the words as they can and recording the words they have spelled successfully. Initially, the parents asked the children to copy the words, but, after some coaching by the teacher, they began directing the children through clues (for example, "Add one letter to **an** and see if you can spell **can**."). The parents report that homework time is now much easier for them and their children.

Alyssa brings home the same list of words as Linda and James. Her parents read each word, and Alyssa uses the color encoding system to tell them the beginning letter. Alyssa's parents are delighted to have a role in supporting her academic progress and are learning how better to interpret her eye gaze at the same time.

 Break/Snack (15 minutes)

15 minutes

 Math (45–60 minutes)

45–60
minutes

Children with Disabilities: Reading and Writing the Four-Blocks® Way • CD-104235 • © Carson-Dellosa

Overview: Sample Day

Children with Disabilities: Reading and Writing the Four-Blocks® Way • CD-104235 • © Carson-Dellosa

40 minutes

The Writing Block (40 minutes)

Mini-Lesson

The children return to their places on the chairs and floor around the teacher. As she begins the mini-lesson, the teaching assistant is launching the computer writing programs that James and Alyssa will use after the mini-lesson. The teacher again reflects on the beginning of the year when neither the assistant nor she knew how to use the software that the special education team recommended. She is grateful that her assistant was allowed to attend the special training with her. Learning how to use the software has been important to her as the teacher, since she is the one who must help these children become writers, but having someone else set up the computers while she continues teaching all of the children is a blessing (not to mention help problem solving when the software or computers malfunction!).

As the teacher begins to write on a transparency, she thinks aloud about her topic choice. She mentions several things that have happened over the weekend that might be interesting topics for her, before she settles on spiders. Her goal for this mini-lesson is showing the children how to write using the information they gathered during Guided Reading earlier in the day. Already, the children have become relatively skilled at personal narratives reflecting their own experiences. Some have begun to write fictional pieces about imaginary characters, but only a few have begun to write informational texts. In her last meeting with the SLP who works with James, she learned that James has made great strides in his ability to construct an oral narrative or story, but he continues to struggle with conveying information to others.

The teacher understands clearly the contribution that reading and writing can make to language development. She hopes the work the class has done all year in reading and writing stories has contributed to James's development. She is determined to increase the effort she always makes at this time of year to help children build their skills in reading and writing informational texts.

While the teacher writes about spiders, she shows children how to spell some of the words by sounding them out. As she does so, she comments that she isn't sure if the words are spelled correctly but that she is sure that they will help her remember her ideas. If she decides later that this first draft is something she would like to revise and perhaps publish, she can get help finding the correct spelling for that word. At the same time, she is careful to spell all words from the Word Wall correctly and refers to it often as she writes. She also uses the chart that the children generated during Guided Reading to help spell words.

When she is finished, her paragraph includes some missing capitals and ending punctuation. It also includes one sentence that doesn't make sense. Usually she has stopped including these sentences by this time in the year, but she has noticed that both Linda and James seem to benefit from the daily opportunity to hear and correct the sentences. She begins as always by reading aloud what she has written to see if it makes sense. The class helps her identify the sentence that doesn't make sense, and then either Linda or James helps her improve the

Overview: Sample Day

sentence. Next, she asks for a volunteer to edit the rest of the sample. Many hands are raised, and one boy is selected to go to the overhead with a different colored marker to lead the class.

During the editing phase, Alyssa uses a simple communication device with speech output to remind her classmates of the editing conventions they have learned. She pushes once on the button of an AbleNet Step-by-Step® communication device, and it says, "Does every sentence begin with a capital letter?" The children decide and then guide the leader in fixing the errors. The process continues with Alyssa pressing the button to produce the following messages in this sequence:

"Does every sentence end with a punctuation mark?"

"Do the names of people and places begin with capital letters?"

"Did you circle the words that might be misspelled?"

Sometimes, Alyssa pushes the button twice in a row and her peers have to ask her to slow down and wait. The SLP told the teacher this was good practice for Alyssa in learning to use the device appropriately. Other times, Alyssa smiles or vocalizes in response to her own question, indicating that she understands that some sentences need end punctuation, capitalization, and so on. Alyssa's role in this lesson also creates a natural reason for the conventions to be repeated again and again. By this point in the year, all of the children can recite them without referring to the chart on the wall. They are really excited when they know a new convention is going to be added for Alyssa to share.

Children Write
After the 10-minute Writing mini-lesson, the children disperse across the room to begin their own writing. There are many different activities happening simultaneously in the room with children at various stages in the writing process. The teacher is quite grateful that she has the additional support of the SLP and OT four days a week during the Writing Block. After much discussion, the team decided that the Writing Block provided an ideal natural environment within which to build both Linda's fine motor and language skills as well as James's computer and language skills. Each child receives two half-hour sessions with each specialist each week. The teacher checks in on the children with the same frequency that she checks in on other children in the class with the result being that she has weekly opportunities to see the therapists interacting with the children and learn some of the strategies they use to support and teach Linda and James.

Alyssa works on the computer during the Writing Block. She is working on a skill called scanning. The teacher could not imagine how Alyssa would ever gain any proficiency as a writer given the labor-intensive nature of the scanning process. Now, however, she marvels as she watches Alyssa reach out and press the red button (switch) that is attached with hook-and-loop tape on the left side of her wheelchair tray. Each time she presses the red switch, the computer presents groups of four or five letters. If the letter Alyssa wants appears in the group she hits a green switch that is near her head. Then, she hits the red switch again to hear each

Children with Disabilities: Reading and Writing the Four-Blocks® Way • CD-104235 • © Carson-Dellosa

Overview: Sample Day

of the letters in the group presented individually. When the letter Alyssa wants is presented, she hits the green switch near her head, and the letter is typed into the word processing program. It can take as long as three or four minutes for Alyssa to type a letter, but Alyssa is now selecting dozens of letters during the writing time. The team is eager for the day to arrive when Alyssa's spelling develops sufficiently for them to interpret the meaning of her writing. For now, they are content to give her the opportunity she needs to learn to use the scanning system as a tool for writing in a manner consistent with what they know the rest of the children experienced throughout kindergarten.

Meanwhile, James is excelling with the computer. He continues to have difficulty reading the most basic books the teacher can find, but he can write interesting and lengthy texts given the support of the computer and the therapists who work with him during this time. The software that seems to have helped him the most is a word prediction program. James types the first letter of the word he would like to spell, and the program generates a list of six words that begin with that letter. Since he can't read the words, he moves the mouse arrow over the words to have the computer read them to him. If the word he wants is in the list, he clicks on it with the mouse. If the word is not there, he tries to type the second letter in the word and read the new words that appear. At this point, if the word is not there, James does his best to spell the word the way that he thinks it sounds and then continues writing.

There was a great deal of discussion about using the software to support a beginning writer. The team was concerned that James would miss out on the benefits of invented spelling and using other supports in the room like the Word Wall. However, the team was persuaded to try the software when they discovered that James could not read his own attempts at writing without the software. He needed the software to help him produce enough correctly spelled words to support him in reading and remembering the other words. The adults who work with him remind him to use the Word Wall to check the spelling of words, and he does have the opportunity to spell words by sounding them out when they don't appear on the list.

A compromise has been reached with Linda to use the computer when she is publishing her work. Although her handwriting is very poor as a result of her motor impairments, she insists on writing with paper and pencil like her friends. Perhaps if there were more than two computers in the room, the team would have been more persistent in convincing Linda to use the computer, but Alyssa and James both like and need the computer during writing, so Linda is supported in writing with paper and pencil.

The OT who works with Linda found a chair that is a perfect height for Linda to sit with her back straight and her feet flat on the floor. She also found an adjustable easel that sits on the tabletop and provides the 35° angle that supports Linda in writing. She adapted a standard triangular pencil grip by notching it out at just the right place to support Linda in maintaining a pincer grasp. Finally, she found paper with raised lines. While many of these modifications were discovered through trial and error, together they help Linda produce writing that she and others can read.

Children with Disabilities: Reading and Writing the Four-Blocks® Way • CD-104235 • © Carson-Dellosa

Overview: Sample Day

Author's Chair

All of the children in the class have been assigned a day of the week. On their designated days, they share with the other children in the class something they have finished or are still writing. Linda and James both enjoy sharing their writing with the class. Linda enjoys the limelight and the positive comments she receives from her peers. James seems particularly proud to share the neatly printed stories he writes on the computer. Often he selects portions to read that include difficult words that he was able to spell successfully with the support of the word prediction software. Both children stop writing a few minutes early on the days they will share so that they can practice reading a few times before they read to the group.

When it is Alyssa's turn to share, she uses the talking word processor feature on the computer. The teaching assistant or therapist working with her highlights the piece she has chosen to share and puts the mouse on the read symbol. When Alyssa presses the switch, the computer reads what she has written. Sometimes the children have to ask her to read again since the speech synthesis has a robotic quality, but the natural opportunity to practice activating the switch on command is useful for Alyssa. On days when she is not sharing, she uses a multi-message communication device (for example, Cheap Talk 4 by Toys for Special Children) to make comments that would fit most writing pieces. Since the comments are not topic specific, this activity provides a good opportunity for Alyssa to attempt to select from an array of choices using her hand. For example, her device is currently programmed to say these three messages:

"I like the ending. What happens next?"

"The middle part was good. What else could you add?"

"I want to know more."

Lunch/Recess (45–60 minutes)

45–60
minutes

Social Studies or Science (45 minutes)

45 minutes

Children with Disabilities: Reading and Writing the Four-Blocks® Way • CD-104235 • © Carson-Dellosa

Overview: Sample Day

**30–45
minutes**

Special (Art, Music, P. E., etc.) or Social Studies/Science Continues (30–45 minutes)

30 minutes

The Self-Selected Reading Block (30 minutes)

When the teacher reads aloud each afternoon, it provides an opportunity for Alyssa to get out of her wheelchair and lounge with her friends on the floor. The students love the fact that Alyssa's presence means they, too, get to lie down on the floor. Initially the teacher worried that she might not have the children's attention if they weren't sitting, but the children have learned to be still and listen. They have learned that they must watch out for each other's safety—particularly Alyssa's, since she is unable to protect herself if a foot or elbow comes her way. The teacher has also learned that Linda and James are most attentive during teacher read-aloud when they sit close to her and can clearly see any illustrations or pictures. On most days, James sits in his child-sized rocking chair right next to the teacher where it is safe for him to rock without bumping the other children, and Alyssa sits on her carpet square right by the teacher's side.

Independent Reading

During independent reading, Linda and James participate in the same way as their peers. They select books from the same bins that their peers use. The teacher has included more beginning level books in all of her bins this year and encourages, but doesn't require, Linda and James to select them. On different days, Linda and James will read with peers, read electronic books individually on the computer, or read with an adult. These alternatives not only support the children's successful reading, but also help them stay on task while minimizing interruptions to the other students. These alternate forms of reading are chosen by the children as desired or by the teacher as needed. Sometimes other classmates read on the computer or with an adult as well.

Alyssa reads independently by reading electronic books on the computer. The electronic books come from three sources: the adapted books from the multiple-copy library at the school, commercially available electronic books, and Alyssa's favorite, electronic books created by the older students in her school who were learning to make multimedia presentations during computer class. The fifth-grade students were using PowerPoint® and had the option of writing or recreating children's books for their final assignment. When the students realized that Alyssa actually needed the books in order to read independently, most of them decided to recreate books rather than other kinds of projects.

Overview: Sample Day

Conferencing

Finding a means to conference with Alyssa has been quite difficult. The teacher is accustomed to listening to children read aloud in order to assess their developing skills as readers. However, Alyssa cannot read aloud—in fact, it is not clear that Alyssa can read at all conventionally. The team continues to seek meaningful ways in which to help Alyssa select books at an appropriate level and to monitor progress in reading. During conferences, she uses her eye gaze to show the teacher the book that is her favorite. The teacher then asks a question that will lead Alyssa to find a particular page in the book. The question might be as simple as, "Show me the page you liked the best." It might focus on words, "Show me a page that has some words you would like help reading." The question might also focus on content, "Show me that page where the dog finds the snake."

Daily Summary and
School-Home Connections (15 minutes)

15 minutes

The teacher has scheduled her daily summary before centers for several years. She was finding it increasingly frustrating to have a meaningful end to the day when children were leaving with parents and heading to the buses on a staggered schedule. Now, she has the summary before centers, and children leave to go home from the centers. This year, the decision to hold the daily summary meeting before centers seems essential.

An important component of the daily summary is reviewing the day and helping the children recall what they learned so that they can talk about it with their families. As the teacher leads the children in discussing what they have learned, Linda selects pictures from a felt board that represent all of the day's activities. She puts the pictures one at a time into pages of the pocket sized photo album that she carries to and from school in her backpack. As each picture is added, she turns the page and adds another. Linda uses this set of pictures as a visual reminder when she talks with her parents each day about what she has learned in school.

Alyssa listens carefully to the wrap-up each day and selects from all of the activities the one activity that she most would like to share with her parents. She chooses from a set of pictures displayed on the piece of clear acrylic attached to the end of her wheelchair tray. Today, Alyssa selects the picture for science by looking at it. As she selects it, the teacher and children remember Alyssa's interest and delight when they all looked on the computer screen and saw the spider that was under the lens of the microscope that had been attached to the computer. Alyssa's partner, who also remembered the incident, volunteers to record a message for Alyssa on her BIGmack® (AbleNet, Inc.). She holds down the button and says, "Today, I got to see a real spider on the computer. It was gross!" She hands the BIGmack® to Alyssa to try. Alyssa presses the switch and smiles broadly as she hears what she will be able to share with her parents when she gets home.

Children with Disabilities: Reading and Writing the Four-Blocks® Way • CD-104235 • © Carson-Dellosa

O v e r v i e w :   S a m p l e   D a y

Alyssa's classmate turns off the BIGmack® (AbleNet, Inc.) and puts it in Alyssa's backpack along with a resealable plastic bag that contains the materials for the Making Words lesson her parents will complete with her for homework. The teacher hands James and Linda their word lists to put in their bags with the Making Words letters that all of the children will use for their homework. The daily summary ends as the teacher guides the class in identifying the new words that were added to their take-home Word Walls this week and reminds them to read for 15 minutes at home this evening.

30–40 minutes

Centers (30–40 minutes)

The last part of every day is spent working at centers. The children choose from centers that are available all year (for example, writing, listening, art, puzzles, board games, reading) and some that are added at particular times to provide additional opportunities to explore curricular areas (for example, a spider display with magnifying glass and identification guide), holidays, and other themes. For the most part, children select their own centers; however, each center can only accommodate a few children at any one time. For years, the teacher has used a ticket system to manage the centers. Each center had a certain number of tickets and children selected a ticket based upon the day of the week to which they were assigned.

This year, the teacher has added pictures and labels to the tickets to represent each of the centers to assist Linda, James, and Alyssa in better understanding the centers they were choosing. In addition to selecting the tickets at the beginning of center time, children now return to the board to exchange tickets in order to explore new centers. This provides the additional support that Linda and James require to avoid wandering from one center to another, and it supports all of the children in planning their time independently.

Overview: Sample Day

Sample Four-Blocks Day in a Special Education Classroom

15 minutes

Opening (15 minutes)

Twelve children who have a variety of disabilities enter and receive any necessary assistance in taking off their coats and using the bathroom. Two teacher assistants collect student books and home-school journals. As they collect the books, the teacher assistants talk briefly with each student marking with a clip any notes in the home-school journal that could or should be shared during morning group.

The books and home-school journals are an important part of the literacy program in the class. Every night, children bring home a book from the classroom's library of adapted books. The adaptations have been designed to promote independent use of the books by the students and facilitate their interactions during reading with parents and other family members. The adaptations of the books include:

- laminated book pages that preserve the life of the book for children who have fine motor difficulties

- page puffers that separate the pages just slightly making it easier for children with physical difficulties to turn the page

DIRECTIONS FOR LAMINATING A BOOK

We start with a paperback version of the book. Depending on the thickness and design of the book, either remove the staples or cut off the binding using a paper cutter. Run each page individually through the laminator. If you disassembled the book by removing staples, staple the book back together. If you cut the binding, use clear packing tape to tape the pages back together. We find this process is easiest when we put two pages next to each other flat on a table and run tape along the seam. Then, we turn the page, put the next page flat on the table, and run a new piece of tape along the seam. Once all of the pages have been reassembled in this way, we use one last piece of tape to cover the binding.

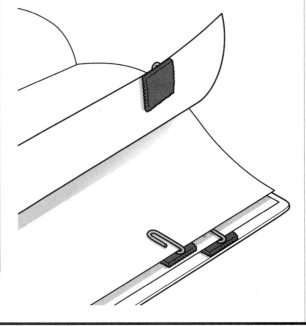

Children with Disabilities: Reading and Writing the Four-Blocks® Way • CD-104235 • © Carson-Dellosa

Overview: Sample Day

- a communication board that includes picture symbols and words that will enable children with communication impairments to talk about the book with others

 red hen

 see

 Red Hen book

 turn the page

 cat

 goose

 loaf of bread

 dog

 teacher

 children

 wheat

 bake

- a visual and written representation of American Sign Language (ASL) that matches the content of the book

Cat
With index finger and thumb touching, move hand out and away from mouth as if holding a cat's whiskers.

Dog
pat
pat
With right hand, pat hip two times and bring hand up to snap fingers.

Children
With palm of right hand open and facing down, move hand upward as if patting the heads of children.

See
Using index and middle fingers on right hand, point at your eyes and then turn hand and move it away.

DIRECTIONS FOR MAKING PAGE PUFFERS

Page puffers can be permanent or removable depending on the age and needs of the child. (There is a choking hazard with removable page puffers.) In either case, they serve to separate the pages of a book so that they can be turned more easily. The easiest form of permanent page puffers are made with stick-back foam weather strip. We usually buy the ¾" (1.9 cm) variety and cut pieces about 1 1/2" (3.8 cm) in length. Then, we remove the backing and stick it to the upper or lower right hand corner of the book page. To make removable page puffers, we use the same foam. We cut ¾" (1.9 cm) strips of tagboard and place paper clips at 2" (5 cm) intervals across the strip. We cut the foam in lengths to match the strips of tagboard. After all of the paper clips are in place, we remove the backing from the weather strip and place it on the tagboard. Finally, we cut the now attached weather strip and tagboard in between the paper clips. The resulting removable page puffers can be attached to the pages of any book to make them easier to turn.

Overview: Sample Day

- a set of magnetic letters and a blank Making Words homework sheet

- a few quick tips for family members regarding how they can promote their child's participation in reading the book

The home-school journals include messages written by the children, their parents, and the adults on the educational team. Families are encouraged to help their children collect remnants, such as movie tickets, napkins from restaurants, and photos from outings and exciting events in their lives. These remnants are included in the home-school journal, and children are encouraged to write about the remnants. Since these children often have difficulty communicating about their experiences, these visual reminders cue teachers about links they can help students make between home and school.

The children also sign in on a chart that is on an easel and indicate whether they have brought their lunch from home or will be buying lunch. Even though several of the children cannot spell their names, they are encouraged to write without copying a model, providing the teacher with an ongoing record of their independent writing development and instructional needs. Sometimes the chart includes other questions that encourage the children to interact with each other or with the adults in order to read a prompt and write a short response.

15 minutes

Group Time (15 minutes)

During group time, the teacher uses the sign-in sheet and home-school journals to structure her interactions with the students. She asks children to read and share new information in the home-school journal. She uses the sign-in sheet to take attendance and models writing on an adapted version of the lunch count form. The original form was designed for ease of reporting, not teaching children to read and write, and it required only that numbers of hot and cold lunches be entered in boxes. When asked, the cafeteria workers were happy to support children's learning with a different form. The children now have practice reading the sign-in chart, counting the entries, and then working with the teacher to write on a transparency a few short lunch count sentences like: "Today, five children will buy chicken nuggets for lunch. One child wants a peanut butter and jelly sandwich."

The teacher is careful to incorporate print whenever possible into group time. All nursery rhyme and poetry texts, as well as song lyrics, are printed on chart paper. When the class reviews the schedule for the day, including any important changes, the children write their personal versions of the schedule. Some of the children write their schedules by selecting from picture symbols that represent the activities. Then, they put them in the correct sequence in a clear plastic pocket chart that the teacher picked up from a baseball card collectors' shop. Other children put the symbols in order and then write the words on the appropriate plastic pockets with grease pencils. Still other children have a single sheet of paper on which they write a words-based schedule. This paper is then slipped into a page protector so that it survives repeated use throughout the day.

Children with Disabilities: Reading and Writing the Four-Blocks® Way • CD-104235 • © Carson-Dellosa

Overview: Sample Day

The Guided Reading Block (30 minutes)

30 minutes

After group time, the children begin the Guided Reading Block. During Guided Reading, the physical therapist (PT) works with Tara, a girl with spina bifida who needs to get out of her wheelchair and into a standing frame each morning. The teacher and therapist observed Tara carefully before deciding that Guided Reading was a good time to use the standing frame. Tara is highly motivated and interested in the interactions that occur during these lessons. Because she is so engaged in the lesson, she often forgets that she is standing, an exercise she resists a great deal. The therapist also noticed that Tara's fine motor control is diminished slightly when she is in her standing frame, but the Guided Reading Block requires far less motor control than the Working with Words Block, which is also interactive and engaging for her.

On most days, the class engages in the shared reading of a big book. Because there is a wide range of abilities within the class, the teacher has found that shared reading is her most effective option—it is the most multilevel of all of the Guided Reading formats. On Thursdays and Fridays, the SLP joins the class during the Guided Reading Block. She continues with shared reading for the five children who are just beginning to use their communication devices at the end of the third day's reading in order to participate more actively in the shared readings. Meanwhile, the teacher guides the other seven children in reading selections from the school's literature collection.

The shared reading of the big book *Mouse Paint* by Ellen Stoll Walsh (Harcourt Big Books, 1991) begins on Monday with a picture walk. In the picture walk, the teacher leads children in looking at the cover of the book, the title, the author, and the illustrator. Children who have speech talk about the cover, while the teacher and assistants help children who do not have speech explore the vocabulary that is available to them on their communication devices. This vocabulary includes the core vocabulary that is always available and the new vocabulary that has been added to reflect key concepts in the new book. Andrea has very limited physical abilities but can use her eyes to point to pictures placed on a piece of 24" x 24" (60.96 cm x 60.96 cm) clear acrylic mounted vertically on her wheelchair tray. Andrea has a total of nine pictures: six pictures represent the primary colors in the book, one picture represents, "I like," one picture allows her to say, "How about you?" and the last picture allows her to say, "I have something to say that is not on my board." The aide sitting on the opposite side of her wheelchair tray interprets as Andrea eye points to the pictures and translates Andrea's communications for other group members to hear.

Another child has a sophisticated, computerized communication system with speech output. A group of picture symbols, with words below each symbol, have been added to his device to represent the specific vocabulary from the story (for example, the primary colors in the book, "mouse/mice," "I like," "How about you?"). The adults also help him remember that he has a set of generic comments about the shared reading that he can access by pushing the correct button. A third child uses ASL to communicate. His physical and cognitive impairments have prevented him from becoming fluent using ASL, but he is able to learn a few new signs each

Children with Disabilities: Reading and Writing the Four-Blocks® Way • CD-104235 • © Carson-Dellosa

Overview: Sample Day

week within the context of the repeated shared reading of the big books. The SLP prepares "cheat sheets" for the adults in the room with three or four ASL signs diagrammed.

During the picture walk, all of these alternative forms of communication are explored and introduced with a great deal of modeling from the adults in the room. The picture walk also provides an opportunity for the teacher to assess and build background knowledge with respect to the particular book. In addition to the remnants that are collected and described in the home-school journal, the teacher sends home short descriptions of upcoming units and books. She asks parents to help her identify experiences that the students have had related to the story content. Because most of the students have communication and/or language impairments, sharing past experiences and making links between personal experiences and school experiences is difficult. With the information provided by parents, the teacher gains information with which to support children in making those important connections.

After the picture walk, the teacher reads the book with the children. The big books that the teacher selects are highly predictable based on the pictures, the print, or repeated text patterns. After a first reading of many big books, children recognize the pattern of the text and can fill in when the teacher pauses or even read along with her. In other books, the pictures help the children predict what the words are saying, and the teacher guides the children in identifying the important pictures and checking to make sure their predictions make sense.

The teacher has found that children respond quite well both to commercially available big books and to books that she makes herself. A favorite format for homemade big books is the *I Like* poem. In these books, the teacher selects a noun that is related to the current unit of study, for example, mice. Then, she creates her own simple book *I Like Mice*:

> I like red mice,
> Blue mice,
> Green mice too.
> I like purple mice. How about you?
>
> I like yellow mice,
> Orange mice,
> Brown mice too.
> I like pink mice. How about you?
>
> I like black mice,
> White mice,
> Silver mice too.
> I like rainbow mice. How about you?

The text of the book is augmented with colorful mice produced on the school's die cast template and cutter. Each phrase or line from the poem appears on a separate page.

After the picture walk, the teacher reads through the book, encouraging children to read with her. On the second reading, the teacher hands each child a colorful mouse or an index card

Children with Disabilities: Reading and Writing the Four-Blocks® Way • CD-104235 • © Carson-Dellosa

Overview: Sample Day

with a color word written on it, depending on the ability of the student. While she reads the book, she encourages children to read with her and asks them to indicate when their cards or mice match the pages.

On the second day, children again use the mice and index cards to contribute to the reading. Then, children make sentences from the book using large word cards. Each child holds a word card, and children rearrange themselves to recreate sentences from the book they have been reading. Children are able to help each other sequence the word cards. As each sentence is made, the teacher guides children to decide if the sentence makes sense. Then, they compare their sentence to the big book or pocket chart. If a sentence does not make sense or does not match, children rearrange it to match the book.

On the third day, the class reads the book together. Children vote on which colorful mice are their favorites, and the teacher writes on a chart as children list all of the things they like that match their favorite colors (for example, yellow: bananas, leaves, Pikachu®, etc.). These lists are later turned into a book called *We Like*. The text begins, "We like yellow leaves, red fire engines, green apples . . . " and continues until all of the items are listed. The list story ends with, "How about you?" Children's drawings and magazine pictures are added to support independent, follow-up readings later.

On the fourth and fifth day, five children continue with shared readings of *I Like Mice* with the SLP. The other seven children read *Mouse Paint* with the teacher. She begins with a picture walk, examining the cover and reading the author's name before previewing all of the illustrations with children. As they look at each picture, they talk about what they think is going to happen in the story and name the things they see. After the picture walk, two pairs of children read the book as partners while the teacher assists the other three children in reading the book. Today, one of the classroom aides checks in on the partners reading independently. Tomorrow, that aide will read with the group of three while the teacher checks in on the other four.

The Working with Words Block (30 minutes)

Working with Words follows the Guided Reading Block. In general, the activities in this Block are designed to help children automatically recognize and spell high-frequency words that they encounter often in their reading and writing. Working with Words activities also teach them to look for patterns in words that will allow them to decode and spell words that they have not been taught to read directly.

30 minutes

In this class, Working with Words is especially designed to build the receptive and expressive vocabulary of children with the most significant communication and language impairments. Every day, the teacher uses the Word Wall as the primary means of instruction in this Block. She also uses a second activity that varies from day to day and focuses on decoding and spelling.

Overview: Sample Day

Word Walls

The five new words that are added to the Word Wall each week are always programmed into communication devices and added to Andrea's communication system. The words are written in black on white cards that are cut to highlight the shape of the word. These white cards are mounted on colorful construction paper. Children with severe communication impairments using symbol-based communication systems are taught to use the symbols to support them in saying the whole word quickly, but they are asked to spell the words letter by letter when the other children clap, chant, and write the words. Andrea uses a Word Wall eye-gaze board like Alyssa's (page 14).

Clapping and chanting the spelling of the words is an important component of the Word Wall activities. Since many of the children in the class have no speech or speech that makes chanting quite difficult, the teacher does silent chants. After modeling the verbal chant and encouraging children who are able to chant with her, she does the same chant in her head while prompting the children to chant in their heads, as well. This direct reference to an inner voice is an important part of all literacy instruction for the children in this class. Children without the ability to speak must be told and encouraged to mimic the actions of their speaking peers and hear the words and sounds in their heads.

The children in this class write the words in a variety of ways. Most of the children have motor delays that limit their ability to write with a pencil. There are not enough computers in the class for all of the children to use a computer. Some children must use the computer every day because handwriting is not possible. Other students write with a pencil some days and on the computer other days. Three days a week, the OT works with children during the Working with Words Block on computer access and handwriting skills. Since the teacher is leading the lesson, the OT can support three or more children at the same time. She makes adjustments to their chairs and tables to make sure they are able to maintain a supportive posture. For the children who are using pencils and paper, she adds triangular grips to their pencils, slanted easels to their desktops, raised lines to their paper, and makes other adjustments that will improve the quality of their handwriting while helping them develop their fine motor strength and coordination. For children who are using the computer, she adds keyguards that decrease the number of accidental key hits, selects software that speaks the letters the children type, adds wrist weights that steady a shaking hand, positions the head stick in exactly the right position with respect to the slant of the keyboard, and often recommends alternative keyboards that provide larger targets and different key layouts from the standard keyboard.

Children with Disabilities: Reading and Writing the Four-Blocks® Way • CD-104235 • © Carson-Dellosa

Overview: Sample Day

Making Words

After completing the Word Wall activity, the children complete a second activity in the Working with Words Block. Today, they will do a Making Words lesson. The children have a great deal of difficulty manipulating the letters that the first-grade teachers use down the hall, but the teacher has discovered several variations. Some children use magnetic letters with a metal cookie sheet and add a star to indicate that they know a letter should be capitalized. Other children have sticky notes that they move around on a white board. Andrea has sticky notes attached to a clear acrylic eye-gaze frame. The notes can be pulled off and placed in the sequence of selection on a white board or other surface that an adult holds. As the teacher gives clues to change just one letter, the adult working with Andrea asks, "Which letter do you need to change?" Then, she points to each letter in the current word and waits for Andrea to indicate with a nod that she is pointing to the letter that must be changed. Then, Andrea selects the replacement letter from the eye-gaze frame. When the letters in a word have to be rearranged to make a new word, the adult partner asks, "Which letter will come first?" and points to each letter in the previous word while waiting for Andrea to indicate, "That one" by nodding slightly.

The boy with the computerized system has an on-screen computer display with only the letters for any given Making Words lesson, a shift key, a delete key, and left and right arrows. Displays similar to this are also created for the alternative keyboards so that some children can use the computer to complete the Making Words lessons.

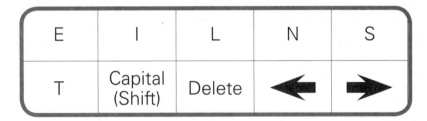

E	I	L	N	S
T	Capital (Shift)	Delete	←	→

Instead of having children go up to the board or the pocket chart to use large cards to make the model for the class to use for self-correction, the teacher has a pocket chart on wheels. She rolls the pocket chart to the child, who then selects the correct letters to make the word and then puts the index card with the word printed on it in a pocket on the bottom half of the pocket chart.

Break/Snack (20 minutes)

20 minutes

Overview: Sample Day

Math (45 minutes)

45 minutes

The Writing Block (30 minutes)

The Writing Block comes at a point in the day when all of the children with physical impairments have had a chance to get their bodies moving but are not yet fatigued. In past years, the Writing Block has had to be the very first Block in the morning to accommodate the children with the most significant physical disabilities who became quickly fatigued during the day. This year, the students seem to have benefited from a few hours of school including sessions with the PT or OT prior to being asked to write.

30 minutes

After a mini-lesson, the children all write using a variety of adapted pencils, computers, and alternative keyboards. All of the children have access to the entire alphabet even if it is not clear that they know all of the letters. In addition to the alphabet, several children also have pictures or other symbols that they can use to compose text. For the children on the computers with alternative keyboards, the alphabet is surrounded by symbols, words, and pictures that they might want to use in their writing; however, all of the children are encouraged to use letter-by-letter spelling each time they write.

Lunch/Recess (60 minutes)

60 minutes

Social Studies or Science (45 minutes)

45 minutes

Children with Disabilities: Reading and Writing the Four-Blocks® Way • CD-104235 • © Carson-Dellosa

Overview: Sample Day

30–45 minutes

Specials (Art, Music, P. E., etc.) (30–45 minutes)

30 minutes

The Self-Selected Reading Block (30 minutes)

This Block begins each day with the teacher reading aloud. At the beginning of the school year, several of the children had a very difficult time sitting and listening while the teacher read. Rather than stop reading, the teacher selected books that were most likely to hold the attention of her children. For example, she selected books that were written to the tune of a song, books that had flaps or textured pages and other interactive components, and other types of reading materials that were short and engaging because of their rhythm, rhyme, predictability, and length.

After listening to the teacher read, the children select books to read independently. There is a large collection of adapted books in the classroom. All of the books in the classroom library have been laminated so that the children can more successfully and independently turn the pages. Many electronic books are available on the computer. Some are commercially available books, and others have been created by a group of students from the local college working on a community service project. There are also books available in slide form that can be read with the aide of an adapted slide projector and a remote switch. The books that children read during Self-Selected Reading are not the same as the books they bring home to read with their families. The creation of an adapted book library has clearly been a priority for this teacher over the years.

Every day at the end of the Block, children are encouraged to share with each other the books they are reading.

10 minutes

Daily Summary and School-Home Connections (10 minutes)

Several of the students in this class require quite a bit of time at the end of the day to get their coats on, pack their bags, and get out to the bus. To accommodate these different needs, the teacher holds her end of the day meeting before the children begin working at centers. Holding the meeting before center time also provides a clear transition from the teacher-directed portion of the day to the child-directed portion.

Overview: Sample Day

The teacher begins by reviewing the schedule with the children and discussing with them the events from the day. The children take their personal schedules home to assist them in talking with parents about their day. The children also collect their home-school journals, which one of the aides or the teacher has written in during Self-Selected Reading. Children are encouraged to write anything they'd like to share in the home-school journal, and the teacher's messages to parents in the journal are shared aloud with children at this time.

Finally, the children select book bags to take home with them. They pull the sign-out cards out of the front of the books, sign their names, stamp them with the date, and deposit the cards in a file box. If a child selects a book that others want, then the others write their names on a waiting list with the title of the book. As children select books, the teacher comments about others who have really enjoyed it, special features in the adaptations, content that is related to events from earlier in the day, and other information that might make the book interesting.

30–40 minutes

Centers

The therapists who work with the students during the school day play an important role in planning the centers. They make sure that the centers address IEP goals that are not addressed during other parts of the day. As in the general education classes, there are some centers that are available throughout the year and others that are available for shorter periods of time. While children are encouraged to visit many different centers during any given week, they are not told which centers to choose or when to rotate to another center. The one rule is that they must communicate their choice for the first center they visit each day. The therapists who work in the room during this time have become particularly skilled at engaging children in centers that they might otherwise avoid because they appear too challenging or novel. Familiar pictures, favorite technologies, preferred social groupings, and other lures are employed to entice the children.

The teacher uses this time to work with individual children or small groups of children who have missed parts of lessons because of equipment failure. The teacher remembers how the disciplinary challenges of her first class gave her an appreciation for computer reboot time she had not held in her teacher education program. Likewise, she uses this time to work with children who have missed parts of activities due to transition time. (For example, getting a child out of a standing frame and into a wheelchair can take as long as five minutes—enough time to miss part of an important Writing mini-lesson or the picture walk in a new book.) She might also provide direct instruction in an area that is proving particularly challenging for a child or varied practice for a child who has not quite grasped a concept that the rest of the class is building on.

Children with Disabilities: Reading and Writing the Four-Blocks® Way • CD-104235 • © Carson-Dellosa

Overview: Sample Day

during the Self-Selected Reading Block, teachers are focused primarily on supporting students in making choices about the materials they read and the way they will respond to their reading. Teachers guide students as they select materials that are appropriate for their reading levels without interfering with true choice. Students with disabilities may have reading levels significantly below other children in the classroom, which makes selection of materials a real challenge. Students with disabilities may also have fine motor, vision, behavior, or attention differences that make selecting, reading, and responding to materials challenging.

Teachers in classrooms with students who have disabilities seek meaningful ways to support children's independent selection and reading of materials. They explore alternative text types and technology supports for their students. They are aware that students don't want to read materials that look dramatically different than those of classmates. They consider the power of popular song lyrics, poetry, and other short texts as options for children who require easy texts to achieve independence.

Self-Selected Reading is important for children with disabilities because it builds fluency and a love for reading. During this time, teachers do not require children to read and respond, but rather set up environments where children want to read and respond.

Self-Selected Reading

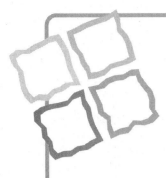

Purposes of the Self-Selected Reading Block

The purposes of Self-Selected Reading are to:

- help students develop the skills to select reading materials that they find interesting

- provide opportunities for students to share and respond to what they are reading

- provide opportunities for teachers to conference individually with children about the books they are reading

- read aloud to children from a wide range of texts and text types

How This Block Matters to Children with Disabilities

The Self-Selected Reading Block is critical for children with disabilities. Without the opportunity to learn that reading is an interesting and enjoyable activity that they can do successfully and independently, skills-based instruction is seldom generalized. Many children with disabilities experience difficulties applying the skills they have been taught across tasks and environments. Self-Selected Reading provides them with a daily opportunity to practice new skills and understandings across tasks, texts, and environments.

Children who experience attention difficulties require Self-Selected Reading in order to develop habits and strategies that will allow them to attend to, enjoy, and understand gradually longer texts. One boy we know found that he was able to focus and attend for longer periods of time when he was sitting in a chair with his own legs wound through the legs of the chair. Another found that listening to classical music through headphones enabled him to sustain his reading. Another girl listened to the story through headphones as she simultaneously read and walked around the room. Without repeated opportunities to read materials of great personal interest, none of these children would have been motivated to independently discover these important and useful self-regulation strategies.

Disabilities affect students' abilities to engage in Self-Selected Reading in a variety of ways. Some disabilities make it impossible for some beginning readers to read aloud like their peers without disabilities. Other disabilities may make it impossible to handle books or to see standard print, so choices are consequently restricted to adapted texts. Some disabilities restrict a student's range of experience, which, in turn, often limits reading interests. No matter the challenges, you must continue to address the goal of Self-Selected Reading for all students.

Children with Disabilities: Reading and Writing the Four-Blocks® Way • CD-104235 • © Carson-Dellosa

Self-Selected Reading

The Self-Selected Reading Block includes the following:

- Teacher Read-Alouds
  The teacher begins the Block by reading aloud to the children from a wide variety of literature, text forms, and technologies.

- Mini-Lessons
  Teachers assist students with disabilities in learning how to find books of interest and use strategies and technologies to read and share more independently.

- Children Reading "On Their Own Levels" from a Variety of Books
  Books in the classroom library include books related to themes the class is studying, easy and hard library books, old favorites, wordless picture books, student-authored texts, easily predictable books, and others. Beyond providing the widest possible range of genres and levels, teachers also incorporate the use of computers to make reading and sharing more accessible to children with disabilities and to provide an engaging alternative for all students.

- Teacher Conferencing with Students
  While the children read, the teacher conferences with a few children each day so that she can also observe and provide the support some children will need to grow in their independent reading.

- Opportunities to Share What They Are Reading with Their Peers
  Teachers, recognizing the communication and learning differences that make talking about text difficult, work with children and related services personnel to help students find ways of sharing their reading interests with others.

Self-Selected Reading

Self-Selected Reading in classrooms with children who have disabilities often looks a little different from the typical Four-Blocks classroom. Often, there are more computers and other technologies in use to increase access to and independence with materials. More often, pairs of children are reading together to support the engagement and success of students who struggle with early reading. Teachers find that conferencing with fewer students each day enables them to support the children requiring more guidance in becoming independent readers.

Children with Disabilities: Reading and Writing the Four-Blocks® Way • CD-104235 • © Carson-Dellosa

Self-Selected Reading

Teacher Read-Aloud

Many teachers recognize the importance of reading aloud to their students. From very early in childhood, listening and interacting while others read is an important source of vocabulary development and knowledge of the world. In addition, reading aloud to students can promote a love of reading and wider reading interests. For children whose disabilities have made it difficult for them to request bedtime stories from their parents or to attend to or understand texts, or whose lives have been filled with concerns for their physical well-being, teacher read-alouds take on even more importance.

About five to ten minutes of every Self-Selected Reading Block is devoted to the teacher read-aloud. This is the time during which the teacher introduces children to a wide variety of text types. While special educators have often been in the habit of reading the same text to children in order to increase comprehension, in Four-Blocks classrooms, they reserve those repeated readings for the Guided Reading Block. Teachers with students who have disabilities need to be particularly diligent about introducing all kinds of texts during these read-alouds and introducing each book thoroughly. They need to recognize that gaps in experience and understanding impact not just understanding, but also appreciation and enjoyment of good literature. Teachers with students who have disabilities need to be particularly conscious of reading aloud plenty of nonfiction, since some students with disabilities find these text structures easier to understand.

Variations in Read-Aloud Materials

In addition to reading from a wide variety of text types and difficulty levels, it is essential that teachers with students who have disabilities read aloud from books that include characters with disabilities. These books provide opportunities for different students to identify more closely with the story, to see disability of a particular type as just one of many individual characteristics, and to become more accepting of individual differences. We have included a list below of books that we have found particularly useful in this regard since they do not focus on disability so much as tell a good story that includes characters with disabilities. We believe this type of text is particularly useful in embracing inclusion.

Read-Aloud Books That Include Characters with Disabilities
Hearing Impairments

- *Dad and Me in the Morning* by Patricia Lakin (Concept Books, 1994)

- *Dina the Deaf Dinosaur* by Carol Addabbo (Hannacroix Creek Books, 1998)

- *I Have a Sister: My Sister Is Deaf* by Jeanne Whitehouse Peterson (HarperCollins, 1977)

- *Moses Goes to the Circus* by Isaac Millman (Farrar, Strauss, and Giroux, 2003)

- *Moses Goes to a Concert* by Isaac Millman (Farrar, Strauss, and Giroux, 1998)

- *Moses Goes to School* by Isaac Millman (Farrar, Strauss, and Giroux, 2000)

- *A Picture Book of Helen Keller* by David Adler (Holiday House, 1992)

Children with Disabilities: Reading and Writing the Four-Blocks® Way • CD-104235 • © Carson-Dellosa

Self-Selected Reading

Visual Impairments

- *Apt. 3* by Ezra Jack Keats (Puffin, 1999)

- *Knots on a Counting Rope* by Bill Martin, Jr., and John Archambault (Henry Holt, 1997)

- *A Picture Book of Louis Braille* by David Adler (Holiday House, 1997)

- *The Secret Code* by Dana Meachen Rau (Children's Press, 1998)

- *Seven Blind Mice* by Ed Young (Philomel, 1992)

- *Through Grandpa's Eyes* by Patricia MacLachlan (Harper Trophy, 1980)

Intellectual Disabilities

- *Be Good to Eddie Lee* by Virginia Fleming (Philomel, 1993)

- *My Friend Isabelle* by Eliza Woloson (Woodbine House, 2003)

- *My Friend Jacob* by Lucille Clifton (Dutton, 1980)

- *Russ and the Almost Perfect Day* by Janet Rickert (Woodbine House, 2001)

- *Russ and the Apple Tree Surprise* by Janet Rickert (Woodbine House, 1999)

- *Russ and the Firehouse* by Janet Rickert (Woodbine House, 2000)

- *We'll Paint the Octopus Red* by Stephanie Stuve-Bodeen (Woodbine House, 1998)

- *Wilfred Gordon MacDonald Partridge* by Mem Fox (Kane/Miller, 1985)

Physical Impairments

- *Bubba and Trixie* by Lisa Campbell Ernst (Simon and Schuster, 1997)

- *Harry and Willy and Carrothead* by Judith Caseley (Greenwillow, 1991)

- *Kelly's Creek* by Doris Buchanan Smith (Crowell, 1975)

- *Mama Zooms* by Jane Cowen-Fletcher (Scholastic, 1993)

- *My Buddy* by Audrey Osofsky (Henry Holt, 1992)

- *Red Riding Hood Races the Big Bad Wolf* by Richard Paul (Twilight Press, 1999)

- *Rolling Along with Goldilocks and the Three Bears* by Cindy Meyers (Woodbine House, 1999)

- *Susan Laughs* by Jeanne Willis (Henry Holt and Company, 2000)

Children with Disabilities: Reading and Writing the Four-Blocks® Way • CD-104235 • © Carson-Dellosa

Self-Selected Reading

Communication or Social Impairments

- *Ian's Walk: A Story about Autism* by Laurie Lears (Albert Whitman and Company, 1998)

- *Silent Lotus* by Jeanne Lee (Sunburst, 1994)

- *Talking to Angels* by Esther Watson (Harcourt Brace, 1996)

Differences

- *The Lonely Scarecrow* by Tim Preston (Dutton Children's Books, 1999)

- *On My Beach There Are Many Pebbles* by Leo Lionni (Mulberry, 1961)

- *Otto Is Different* by Franz Brandenberg (Greenwillow, 1985)

- *The Stranger* by Chris Van Allsburg (Houghton-Mifflin, 1986)

- *Why Am I Different?* by Norman Simon (Albert Whitman and Company, 1976)

Mini-Lessons

Teachers in classes serving students with disabilities find that it is important to teach children various aspects of selecting, reading, and sharing independent reading. However, these teachers also recognize that a little teaching and a lot of experience go a long way.

Selecting

Some students with disabilities, because of their lack of successful experience and a desire to be just like peers, may consistently choose books that are too difficult to read independently. Other students find a book that they can read successfully and stick with it to the exclusion of wider reading. You may find the following strategies to be useful in assisting students to make better choices:

- thinking aloud as they search the shelves for books on particular topics

- "blessing" books by bringing in three to five books on a topic and on an easy level; "selling" each book by reading a short segment, asking a question, or sharing something about the content, before making all of the books available for student reading

- making easy and interesting books available, but only for reading in the most desirable locations (for example, the rocking chair, the bean bag, the moon chair, etc.)

- modeling reading of a random page in a book for interest and ease before choosing it to read

- bringing a few books for individual "blessings" during conferences

Self-Selected Reading

Children with Disabilities: Reading and Writing the Four-Blocks® Way • CD-104235 • © Carson-Dellosa

Reading

Many students with disabilities lag significantly behind classmates in their independent reading abilities. They may find it difficult to make letter-sound connections, to attend to text, to process print visually, to turn pages, or otherwise engage in the behaviors and thinking that make reading a pleasure when done automatically. To promote more independent reading in students who struggle, you may find the following mini-lessons to be useful:

- modeling how to use ReadPlease® (*http://www.readplease.com*) to have the computer read aloud Internet sites and other digital texts of interest

- making sure that students understand that reading is not spinach and that it is okay to put a book down before finishing if it proves to be uninteresting or too difficult

- modeling how to manipulate the various animations and talking text options in the stories at Starfall (*http://www.starfall.com*)

- reading along with students who struggle so that they can experience what good reading feels like

- modeling how to copy and paste a digital text into a talking word processor, such as WriteOut:Loud®, and select a voice (*http://www.donjohnston.com*)

Sharing

Students with communication, cognitive, or learning disabilities may struggle in sharing what they read. They may lack sufficient vocabulary, understanding of story or expectations, or the ability to organize their thoughts. In these cases, you may find the following mini-lessons to be useful:

- modeling how to use Inspiration® (*http://www.inspiration.com*) templates to remember and organize what students want to say about a particular book

- modeling how to use Kidspiration® (*http://www.inspiration.com*) not just to remember and organize, but also to use the talking text feature to share ideas about books

- modeling how to use cue cards with key words, pictures, or symbols to remember or organize what students want to say about a particular book

- modeling how to use writing and a talking word processor instead of speech to share books

- modeling how to use story structure guides to prompt book discussions

Self-Selected Reading

Children Read and Conference with the Teacher

The majority of each Self-Selected Reading Block should be spent reading. During this time there are decisions to be made regarding where children will read, how they will read, what they will read, and whether an individual child will conference with the teacher on a given day. *The Teacher's Guide to the Four Blocks®* (Cunningham, Hall, and Sigmon, 1999) provides an explanation for each of these. Here, we will describe the additional issues to consider when addressing the needs of children with disabilities.

Variations in Where Children Read

In designing a system that determines where children will read in your class, you must take into account the needs of the individual children in your class. You may have to have more children away from their desks than you would prefer in order to ensure that children have enough space to stay engaged in their reading. You may have to have more children sitting in their seats than you would prefer because some students require greater structure. If students are concerned about what is "fair," you'll have to help them understand that individuals need different things in order to have fair opportunities to engage in Self-Selected Reading. The key is to spend the first few days and weeks of school carefully observing and encouraging change so that you can determine which situation is best suited for the child or children you are trying to support.

Variations in How Children Read

Many teachers find technology indispensable for accomplishing their goal that all students independently explore, select, and read a wide array of texts, particularly when they want students to engage in these activities beyond the school day. You may find that you have to devote conscious attention to some children's differences and preferences to reach them. Some children with disabilities enter school unaware of what books are used for or how to use them because of the amount of time they have spent in medical settings or therapeutic programs. Other children with disabilities may have a lesser understanding of the range of possibilities for reading because of their cognitive, visual, or hearing impairments. Some children with disabilities may find it difficult to engage in sustained silent reading in the classroom because of attention or behavior differences. Teachers often find that their school and classroom collection of trade books and magazines simply doesn't meet the needs of students with disabilities. You may find a greater need for books on tape, large print books, digital books, Internet books, and a variety of adaptations to the materials and environment that will enable children with disabilities to begin to understand their personal connections with reading and become lifelong readers.

Children with Disabilities: Reading and Writing the Four-Blocks® Way • CD-104235 • © Carson-Dellosa

Self-Selected Reading

Adapting Trade Book Collections

Books can be physically adapted in a variety of ways to increase the ability of children with disabilities to explore them more independently. Common adaptations include:

- taking apart a book and laminating each page or placing each page in a plastic page protector
  These adaptations protect books from children who might put them in their mouths, from the hard use they can get from children with physical disabilities, or from children who have not yet learned what books are for or how to handle them.

- placing books at a height and angle where they are more easily seen and used by children with physical or visual impairments (for example, on book stands)

- tape-recording books that are read fluently yet slowly for children who are unable to read independently but can follow along as someone else reads
  Many teachers now record a book directly into a computer, burn a CD with the recording, and place it in a pocket in the back of the book. Even children who can read independently sometimes like to listen to a book read aloud or read along with the narrator.

- separating pages so that they are more easily turned by children with physical impairments or fine motor difficulties
  The most common separators include craft sticks, pieces of foam, and packing peanuts that have been attached to paper clips with a hot glue gun. (See page 31.) The separators can be clipped over the pages of any book in seconds and reused with any book the child would like to read. (*http://www.wiu.edu/thecenter/articles/adaptlit.html*)

Some teachers find the BookWorm™ (AbleNet, Inc.; *http://www.ablenetinc.com*) a particularly useful tool for integrating children with severe disabilities into partner reading experiences with classmates and trade books. The text is read into the device page by page, and then page detectors synchronize the reading with the appropriate pages. With the device, children with severe communication impairments or significant intellectual disabilities, can take turns "reading aloud" with partners. The device offers high-quality sound output and headphones as options.

Thoughtful teachers also recognize that books on shelves with only the spines displayed are seldom selected by children without a great deal of experience in picking books. Make sure that many books are displayed on the shelves with the covers showing, on magazine racks, and in various displays around the room. Develop systems so that each month, different books are displayed in this way. Attempt to display every book in the classroom collection one or more times during the year.

Children with Disabilities: Reading and Writing the Four-Blocks® Way • CD-104235 • © Carson-Dellosa

Self-Selected Reading

Using Electronic Texts on the Internet

Electronic text is an important alternative to physically traveling to libraries, selecting books from shelves, and turning pages by hand. Electronic texts offer a wide variety of supports for children who may be struggling with various aspects of independent reading. Some of these texts are accompanied by read-aloud options, some texts are read aloud automatically, and some texts allow the reader to click on individual words if they are unsure how to read them. Some electronic texts are interactive, providing children the option of animating illustrations or modifying the story line (for example, Edmark's Make A Story Web site—*http://www.riverdeep. net/language_arts/edmark_lang_arts/MakeAStory/MakeAStory.html*). Many Web sites offer collections of digital children's texts that can easily be copied, downloaded, and used with some of the software discussed in this chapter, or with talking word processors, to provide children with supports that trade books cannot.

There are many such sites that can be accessed by doing an Internet search for the term "children's electronic books" or "children's electronic texts." Some of the sites that we like to include are Starfall's Learn to Read Web site, which has interactive texts on multiple levels of interest to young readers (*http://www.starfall.com*), and Scholastic's interactive Clifford storybook Web site (*http://teacher.scholastic.com/clifford1/index.htm*). Useful gateway sites with links to a number of these electronic book sites are Eduscape's Electronic Books and Online Reading (*http://eduscapes.com/tap/topic93.htm*) and the Internet Public Library's Kidspace (*http://www.ipl.org/div/kidspace/*). Perhaps the richest online resource, Kidspace has links that take children and teachers to author Web sites, online comics, e-zines, poetry, children's stories in Spanish, and many other engaging resources. Using Read:OutLoud software (*http://www.donjohnston.com*), these Web sites can be read aloud as the text is highlighted.

Two digital book collections created specifically for students with disabilities are Joe Rickerson's Accessible Book Collection (*http://www.accessiblebookcollection.org*) and Benetech's Bookshare. org (*http://www.bookshare.org*). Both are nonprofit organizations offering slightly different collections. Bookshare.org has thousands of digital texts and began as a collection for adults with disabilities and now continues to add digital texts from a wide variety of sources. The Accessible Book Collection has hundreds of titles and continues to grow exclusively as a children's book collection. Both collections offer subscriptions to individuals and schools. Ken Pope provides links to other services offering accessible texts at http://kspope.com/accbooks.

Children with Disabilities: Reading and Writing the Four-Blocks® Way • CD-104235 • © Carson-Dellosa

Self-Selected Reading

Fair Use of Electronic Materials

Downloading or using copyrighted materials from the Internet without permission is against the law. "Fair use" should guide teachers in the use of electronic materials. For example, it is fair for teachers to make digital copies of trade book or textbook materials to enable a child to read them who otherwise could not. It is not fair to download a copyrighted text and make 20 copies for an entire class in which only some of the children have identified disabilities. Schools, as nonprofit agencies, are legally entitled to reproduce, adapt, and distribute copyrighted works if the adapted materials are for the exclusive use of students with print-related disabilities. Bookshare.org (*http://www.bookshare.org*), a fee-based service offering access to digital texts for individuals with disabilities, has a clear explanation of fair use issues in their pages devoted to legal issues (*http://www.bookshare.org/web/Legalities.html*) and frequently asked questions (*http://www.bookshare.org/web/SupportFAQ.html*).

Student-, Teacher-, or Volunteer-Made Electronic Texts

Many teachers make, or guide volunteers in making, electronic books for students. These homemade texts offer greater levels of access and adaptability. On-screen text can often be magnified, displayed in different fonts, displayed with different foreground/background colors, and highlighted to support tracking. Pages can be "turned" with the click of a mouse or even automatically. Web sites can be bookmarked, facilitating independence and control of the material. Images can be viewed with magnification, in color, or higher contrast black and white, mimicking a CCTV. Text material can be cut and pasted for writing tasks, minimizing or eliminating typing.

My Own Bookshelf (SoftTouch, Inc., *http://www.softtouch.com*) is one piece of software that you can use to create a variety of supports for independent reading by children who struggle. The software consists of a set of integrated tools to help teachers easily create electronic books on the computer (Macintosh/PC) that are displayed in bookshelves that offer easy selection for students. Helpful "wizards" allow the user to add digital images, movies, and text. Digital sound files can be imported or recorded, and text can be read aloud by the computer using the synthetic text-to-speech feature. The program is quite user-friendly, with walk-throughs for the process of creating, storing, and selecting books.

The resulting books are stored in the computer in folders (bookshelves) arranged as you wish (for example, by child, by topic, by difficulty level, etc.). When children choose a book to read at the computer, important supports can be offered that regular books don't have. For example, children who cannot read the text because of impaired vision or poor reading skills can listen to the computer read the text aloud as other children look at the text. Children who have difficulty understanding concepts or vocabulary in new materials (for example, a child with intellectual disabilities such as Down syndrome) can read a text that has sound or movie files that enable the reader to see and hear more about the new information. Children who have difficulty attending to tasks have their attention focused and recalled to the text because of the vivid images, sound files, and movies. Additional supports are built in for control of the texts by children with physical impairments.

Self-Selected Reading

Children with Disabilities: Reading and Writing the Four-Blocks® Way • CD-104235 • © Carson-Dellosa

Teachers find the options of tracking how long and how often students choose and use particular books helpful in many ways. Some teachers use the information to guide conferencing discussions about reading interests and habits. Some teachers create additional books on similar topics or with similar features. Some teachers use the information to encourage wider reading.

Read:OutLoud™ Solo Edition (Don Johnston, Inc., *http://www.donjohnston.com*) was created with older students in mind, but offers some unique advantages to teachers in Four-Blocks classrooms. The software allows teachers to create customized electronic texts with illustrations. Some teachers use the software with a scanner to import their existing classroom libraries into electronic forms that support students who may have attention, behavior, vision, or reading difficulties with the read-aloud feature and integrated Franklin Dictionary. Features, such as the highlighting tool, support students in identifying parts of the book to share after reading. Features, such as the Support Reading Guide, can also be used during the Guided Reading and Writing Blocks to help children better understand story structure or content, or to support summary writing.

Other software can be used to create electronic texts, but none offer the ease of storage and access of My Own Bookshelf® or Read:OutLoud™ Solo Edition. Examples of other software that teachers have used to create books include PowerPoint® (Microsoft Corporation, *http://office.microsoft.com/en-us/FX010857971033.aspx*), Appleworks® (Apple Computer, Inc., *http://www.apple.com/appleworks/*), HyperStudio (Sunburst Technology, Inc., *http://www.hyperstudio.com*), KidPix® Studio Deluxe (Brøderbund), and MP Express™ (Bytes of Learning, Inc., *http://www.bytesoflearning.com*). Each piece of software offers teachers the ability to create their own text, import images, record accompanying read-alouds, and integrate sound and movie files. HyperStudio® has been used by schools for many years and is often available to teachers when other software is not. Many teachers like the ease of access to other HyperStudio® creations through the HyperStudio® Connection (*http://www.hyperstudio.com/HyperStudioConnection.aspx*) and Internet searches. Teachers also like the cross-platform supports of MP Express™ and the resource CDs with image, sound, and movie files about endangered animals, Africa, rainforests, and other topics.

Commercial Electronic Texts

Many companies make collections of electronic texts that offer animation, text-to-speech, and other supportive features for struggling readers. SoftTouch has a library of nine animated stories—Running Start Books—about a dragon, a firefighter, a camping trip, and other topics that can be used within My Own Bookshelf or independently with the included Reader software.

The Belevedere-Tiburon Library in California provides links to more than 100 children's books on CD and more than a thousand children's books on tape (*http://www.bel-tib-lib.org/kids/lists/type.htm*). Many of the books on CD allow children to animate different parts of the illustrations and to hear the text read aloud as it is highlighted. Books on tape enable children to engage with text they may be unable to read independently when an adult is unavailable. Additional books on CD can be found by searching the Internet for "children's books on CD."

Children with Disabilities: Reading and Writing the Four-Blocks® Way • CD-104235 • © Carson-Dellosa

Self-Selected Reading

Conference Variations

Teachers in Four-Blocks classrooms who have students with disabilities find the individual conferencing time during Self-Selected Reading to be indispensable. They find that this one-to-one time enables them to help students find books that fit both their interests and abilities. This time helps teachers learn who their students are as readers. Many teachers like to sit facing the rest of the class so that they can also see a clock. By facing the class, teachers can monitor the other students as needed during the conference. By seeing a clock, they can gather informal reading rate information under more natural conditions than when students know that they are being assessed.

One important variation of the conference is that many students with disabilities must be taught how to ask and answer questions. Teachers often begin this process by having a student read aloud a favorite passage from a book he is reading. Then, the teacher engages in reciprocal questioning with the student about the passage, taking turns with the student in asking and answering open-ended questions (Manzo, 1969).

Teachers also teach children question-answer relationships to improve students' ability to answer questions more thoughtfully and completely by identifying the information requested (Raphael and Au, 2005). Types of questions include two broad categories: In the Book questions and In My Head questions. In the Book questions have two categories: Right There—answers that students can find right on the page and Think and Search—answers that students can find on the page but that usually require students to put together a couple of pieces of information. In My Head questions consist of Author and Me—answers that require some information from the text and some information from the reader and On My Own—answers that can be given without even reading the text.

Armed with these strategies, students with disabilities engage in richer dialogue over time not only in reading conferences, but also in Guided Reading lessons.

Variations in Conference Focus

More often than not, teachers find that helping their students with disabilities anticipate the focus of a conference improves the quantity and quality of student interaction during the conference. Many teachers provide these students with a list of questions to consider, a visual diagram to organize the process, or a series of steps that are followed until they become routine. Anything that enables the students to consider their responses prior to sitting down with the teacher usually leads to better use of the conferencing time.

Conference Scheduling and Focus

Teachers often find that they need more than three or four minutes to conference adequately with students with disabilities. These students may take longer to read aloud or respond to questions. They may require prompts to respond to questions, or they may require longer time to process or express their thoughts. Often, especially early in the year, teachers in these classrooms will conference with only two or three students a day. They feel less rushed and are able to use the remaining minutes of silent reading time to monitor, and assist as necessary, all of the students.

Children with Disabilities: Reading and Writing the Four-Blocks® Way • CD-104235 • © Carson-Dellosa

Self-Selected Reading

Book Choices

In Four-Blocks classrooms, teachers use the reading conference to encourage and guide independent reading. Teachers of students with disabilities have a few additional considerations. For example, some students with disabilities will develop favorite books that they read to the exclusion of all other texts. Conferencing can assist teachers in discovering what makes a book a favorite (for example, topic, ease of reading, personal connection to something in student's life, and so on), and then the teacher can expand the repertoire. Other teachers have found that when they provide actual book choices during the conference, or assist the student in searching, the student will select materials of more appropriate difficulty.

Teachers will also assist students with disabilities at this time in exploring technology-supported reading. Some students benefit from seeing and hearing text simultaneously or demonstrate greater interest or attention when materials are presented on a computer. Other students read with greater attention because they can animate illustrations or move through levels of hypertext. Some benefit from features like increasing the text size or manipulating text and background colors. All of these features can be explored over time in individual conferences.

Assessment

Some teachers find conferencing to be an ideal time to gather informal assessment data. For example, teachers will sit so that they can see a wall clock while children read a sample passage from their book. In this way, they can get a good measure of students' natural reading rates. Other teachers will create either a video or audio recording of a child reading aloud. These tapes can be shared with parents at conferences or examined later for miscues, fluency, and reading rate. They can be used to document progress across the year.

We find that teachers are often concerned when they have students who are unable to engage in oral reading as a result of communication impairments. These teachers often ask, "How do I know the child is really reading?" Teachers can use the interactions they have during conferences to gain confidence that the child is successfully reading. The manner in which children respond to and pose questions during conferences provides important insight for teachers. We also find that teachers can spontaneously create modified cloze tasks by covering a word in the book the child is currently reading (using a finger if necessary) and offering three choices of words to complete the sentence. When children successfully identify the target word on four out of five probes, the teacher can have confidence that the child is "really reading."

Children with Disabilities: Reading and Writing the Four-Blocks® Way • CD-104235 • © Carson-Dellosa

Self-Selected Reading

Sharing Variations

It is particularly important for students with disabilities to experience book sharing. Often, because of their differences, these students come to school with fewer experiences with book sharing, less involvement in library reading programs, and limited access to meaningful independent exploration of books.

In such classes, the teacher and an aide or volunteer often begin the year by modeling Reader's Chair for the rest of the students. One adult shows the cover and a favorite illustration, reads a short passage of interest, and then tells students why they might also like to read the book. The other adults model asking good questions.

When students struggle in sharing their reading with peers because of communication impairments or intellectual disabilities, teachers provide picture, symbol, or word cues to support communication or memory. Various story structure forms, as well as text structure templates from Kidspiration or Inspiration (*http://www.inspiration.com*), are used to help students increase their ability to talk about what they've read. One teacher we know helped a boy in her class prepare for sharing by making himself brief notes in the form of letters, words, and very simple pictures just prior to his turn.

Teachers with students with disabilities employ partner and small group sharing more often than in other classes in order to increase the frequency and interactivity of sharing, as well as the comfort of some students in sharing. Teachers of students with disabilities recognize that they often struggle in understanding the meaning of questions or in asking their own questions. They engage students in reciprocal question activities (Manzo, 1969) in both Guided Reading lessons and in Self-Selected Reading mini-lessons to teach them not only how to ask, but also how to answer high-quality questions.

Voice-output technologies like the Step-by-Step (AbleNet, *http://www.ablenetinc.com*) are employed to enable students with severe intellectual disabilities to engage in sharing by activating a sequence of preprogrammed messages about the chosen book.

Making the Self-Selected Reading Block Multilevel

While Self-Selected Reading is inherently multilevel for most children, it requires conscious effort by the teacher to make it multilevel for students with disabilities. If students are to have true choices, then their interests must be represented in the available reading materials, at levels of difficulty they can manage, and in accessible formats. To make the Self-Selected Reading Block multilevel for all students, the teachers should interview students about their interests, collect the widest range of levels, topics, and genres of books possible. The teacher should adapt books to accommodate children's individual differences. The teacher should also incorporate technology use into the Block to further enhance students' independence in selecting, reading, and sharing books.

Children with Disabilities: Reading and Writing the Four-Blocks® Way • CD-104235 • © Carson-Dellosa

Self-Selected Reading

In conferences with children, the teacher should show a genuine interest in their reading and steer struggling readers to personally interesting, easy books. The teacher should demonstrate technology that supports independent reading and sharing. Often, a teacher can interview parents to further identify a student's reading interests. However, teachers should be careful to remember that even students with significant reading difficulties are encouraged, not required, to read books on their levels.

Summary of the Self-Selected Reading Block

The purpose of this Block is to build reading fluency, to support students in becoming more independent in finding and reading texts at their own independent reading levels, and to build confidence in students as readers.

Teacher Read-Aloud/Mini-Lesson

The teacher reads aloud to all students from a variety of genres, topics, and authors, and incorporates texts including characters with disabilities. While reading, the teacher models how he finds books of interest in databases or by searching particular areas of the library. The teacher shows how he finds an appropriately easy and personally interesting book by sampling a page within the book. The teacher demonstrates how to use various technologies for reading and sharing.

Children Read and Teacher Conferences

The teacher holds conferences with two to three children daily as the other children read. This allows her to have more time for monitoring and assisting students who may struggle during independent reading time. She keeps a conference form recording each child's individual progress, preferences (both reading types and technologies), and responses.

Sharing

A few students share briefly (approximately two minutes each) with the class what they like or don't like about what they have been reading. Often, teachers with students with disabilities do this sharing in table groups of four to six students so that more children share more frequently in a lower-pressure situation. In either case, the teacher models asking and answering questions, more frequently supporting the groups with students with disabilities.

Self-Selected Reading

Children with Disabilities: Reading and Writing the Four-Blocks® Way • CD-104235 • © Carson-Dellosa

A Typical Week in the Self-Selected Reading Block
Monday

Teacher Read-Aloud/Mini-Lesson

READ-ALOUD TITLE

A Place for Grace by Jean Davies Okimoto (Sasquatch Books, 1993)

The teacher gathers students around her in the reading area. She reminds students that they have been discussing the many ways they are alike and different. The children, as always, are engaged by this story about a dog and are interested to learn that the dog helps a man who has hearing impairments.

Using the school's LCD projector, the teacher projects her computer on a movie screen and opens up her Web browser to the Starfall electronic books site (*http://www.starfall.com*). She shows them how to choose books from the available categories and how to hear the stories read aloud on the computer. She also shows the students how to find the Web site in the class's I Keep Bookmarks (*http://www.ikeepbookmarks.com*) annotated electronic bookmarks site. Finally, she shows them the sign-up sheet for the computer-based reading center.

Children Read/Teacher Conferences

Students make independent reading selections and settle down to read. Several students have chosen the option of reading with a partner, a choice that supports the attention and engagement of many students with disabilities and that all children enjoy.

The teacher conferences with two students about their books, fewer than she used to do without students with disabilities, but she finds this allows her more time to monitor and support the students Self-Selected Reading success. She gives the students the usual two-minute warning prior to the end of reading time, which she has found helps all of her students transition smoothly, but especially her students with disabilities.

Sharing

The children gather on a carpet in the room, and one child shares her book with the class. The teacher models higher-level questions, asking, "Why did you choose that book to read? Which books does it remind you of?"

Self-Selected Reading

Tuesday

Teacher Read-Aloud/Mini-Lesson

ABC for You and Me by Margaret Girnis (Albert Whitman & Company, 2000)

The teacher gathers students around her in the reading area. She explains that the read-aloud book is an alphabet book, like some that they have been making in the Working with Words Block. The children enjoy the photos and make connections between the letters and many of the objects pictured. In answer to a student question, the teacher notes that the children in the photos all have Down syndrome. Earlier in the year, the parents of some of the students with Down syndrome had led a session on some of their children's differences and how students could be good friends and classmates.

The teacher turns to the in-class library collection and thinks aloud as she searches for a book to read. She notes that she'd really like to read a fairy tale and knows that the fairy tale book section has two words beginning with a capital **F** and a capital **T**. She chooses one of the books, looks at many of the pictures, and comments on how interesting they are, and then reads one page. She says to herself, "I can read these words, and this book looks interesting. I'm going to check it out for Self-Selected Reading time."

Children Read/Teacher Conferences
The students read quietly, individually and in pairs, and two students read along with the talking books at the Starfall Web site while the teacher conferences with the two Tuesday students.

Sharing
Today, students meet at their work tables in groups of four to share summaries of what they are reading, what they like about it, and who they think would like to read it and why.

Wednesday

Teacher Read-Aloud/Mini-Lesson

First half of *The Hickory Chair* by Lisa Rowe Fraustino (Arthur A. Levine, 2001)

The teacher gathers students around her in the reading area. She leads the students in a discussion about grandparents and relatives. She also discusses blindness as another form of difference between people. After reading the first few pages about a boy who is blind and his family, the teacher leads the class in predicting what they think might happen in the rest of the story.

Self-Selected Reading

Children with Disabilities: Reading and Writing the Four-Blocks® Way • CD-104235 • © Carson-Dellosa

Children with Disabilities: Reading and Writing the Four-Blocks® Way • CD-104235 • © Carson-Dellosa

Having noticed that some of the students had difficulty summarizing what they were reading yesterday, the teacher shows students how to use a herringbone to answer important questions about their stories. The bones of a fishlike skeleton on the chart stand read "who, what, where, when, why, how."

Children Read/Teacher Conferences
Students read individually, in pairs, and at the computer as the teacher conferences with the Wednesday students.

Sharing
Students meet at their work tables in groups of four to share summaries of what they are reading, what they like about it, and who they think would like to read it and why. At each table, the teacher places a copy of the herringbone for reference and notices that many students help each other summarize by using the prompts.

Thursday

Teacher Read-Aloud/Mini-Lesson

> **READ-ALOUD TITLE**
>
> Second half of *The Hickory Chair* by Lisa Rowe Fraustino

The teacher gathers students around her in the reading area and leads them in remembering what she read aloud yesterday. She continues reading aloud the remainder of the story.

The teacher has noticed that children seldom choose to read fables in her classroom, so she has brought three wonderful examples to talk about. First, she provides a quick overview of the three examples. Next, she shows students the hilarious illustrations and reads a page from *Squids Will Be Squids* by John Scieszka and Lane Smith (Viking Juvenile, 1998). Finally, she takes the class to a Web site created by an art professor and her students at the University of Massachusetts Amherst (*http://www.umass.edu/aesop/*). She shows students how to access a wonderful collection of animated fables and how to control the speed of presentation with the slider at the bottom of the image window.

Children Read/Teacher Conferences
Students read individually, in pairs, and at the computer as the teacher conferences with the Thursday students.

Sharing
Students meet at their work tables in groups of four to share summaries of what they are reading, what they like about it, and who they think would like to read it and why. The teacher reminds them to continue using the herringbone to summarize their stories.

Self-Selected Reading

Friday

Teacher Read-Aloud/Mini-Lesson

Tuesday by David Wiesner (Clarion Books, 1991)

Today, the teacher shows children a wordless picture book. The class enjoys the fanciful illustrations and collectively "reads aloud" the fantasy tale.

The teacher shows children the free version of ReadPlease (*http://www.readplease.com*) she downloaded to the computer this week. She shows the class how to open digital books at the PBS Between the Lions reading site (*http://pbskids.org/lions/stories.html*) and use ReadPlease to "read-aloud" the stories and definitions.

Children Read/Teacher Conferences
Students read individually, in pairs, and at the computer as the teacher conferences with the Friday students.

Sharing
Two students, who have been reading wordless picture books this week, share their books with the class. The teacher leads the class in asking high-quality questions.

Children with Disabilities: Reading and Writing the Four-Blocks® Way • CD-104235 • © Carson-Dellosa

Self-Selected Reading

Teacher's Checklist for the Self-Selected Reading Block

In preparing and adapting my Self-Selected Reading lessons to make them appropriate for the children with disabilities in my class, I have . . .

_____ 1. Provided a good model of slower, fluent reading so that all of the children can understand and enjoy the read-aloud story. I remembered it's often important to stop in midreading to re-engage wiggly or confused children with a picture or story discussion, or a prediction.

_____ 2. Provided an adequate and wide supply of books and other reading materials, particularly those below grade level, so that all students have something they want to read and can understand.

_____ 3. Made books accessible to children so that they can easily and independently choose and explore books.

_____ 4. Reduced the number of children I typically conference with, especially early in the year, so that I can monitor more closely the independent reading of struggling students, assist with technologies, and explore a variety of supports for students who need them to be successful.

_____ 5. Limited the time spent on each conference to 3–5 minutes and remembered that my goal is fair, not equal, treatment of my students. I have rushed no students, but I have provided greater preparation and processing time for students requiring greater structure to succeed.

_____ 6. Used questions in my conferences, especially with students with disabilities, that let children know what is important about their reading rather than emphasizing minor details. I have modeled both asking and answering questions for students who struggle.

_____ 7. Guided and encouraged students to read books on appropriate levels, while still allowing freedom of choice. I have brought appropriate books of potential interest with me to struggling students' conferences so that they can "try them on."

_____ 8. Promoted reading through teacher read-alouds and book talks and by providing time for students to talk about their reading with each other each day.

_____ 9. Helped children make connections between read-alouds and previous class reading, students' personal interests, and subjects, themes, and concepts the class has studied or will study.

Children with Disabilities: Reading and Writing the Four-Blocks® Way • CD-104235 • © Carson-Dellosa

Self-Selected Reading

IEP Goals for the Self-Selected Reading Block

Goals for the individualized education plan (IEP) in Self-Selected Reading should reflect the skills and understandings that children are expected to develop as they engage in wide reading of books and other materials. Remember that the purposes for the Self-Selected Reading Block (page 42) include helping students develop the skills to select reading materials that they find interesting and providing students with opportunities to share and respond to what they are reading. Teacher conferences serve as the primary means of monitoring students during Self-Selected Reading. Here are some example goals for Self-Selected Reading arranged from the lowest to the highest skill levels.

1. Given daily opportunities to select from a regularly changing assortment of books, the student will successfully choose from an array of books on four out of five days.

2. During the Self-Selected Reading Block, the student will engage in silent study of different features of the book (favorite picture, particular page) at least twice per book.

3. Given age- and ability-appropriate reading materials with Braille and tactile supports/ enhanced pictures, the student will use different hand movements (general touch vs. left to right tracking) as a means of demonstrating an understanding of the difference between print (Braille) and illustrations (tactile supports/enhanced pictures).

4. When reading orally a passage at the <insert level one or more levels higher than current>, the student will accurately identify 97 percent of the words and maintain a <insert target words per minute rate> words-per-minute rate.

5. The student will read a variety of texts at <insert level one or more levels higher than current> with fluency and comprehension.

Children with Disabilities: Reading and Writing the Four-Blocks® Way • CD-104235 • © Carson-Dellosa

Self-Selected Reading

In the Guided Reading Block, teachers are focused primarily on choosing materials for children to read for set purposes. Teachers guide students to use reading strategies needed for the given material and the given purpose. Students with disabilities may have reading levels significantly below other children in the classroom, making selection of materials a real challenge. Students with disabilities may also have behavioral or communication differences that make peer interaction or partner reading difficult.

Teachers in classrooms with students who have disabilities seek meaningful ways to support children's comprehension of text. They explore alternative peer, text, and technology supports for reading and interaction. They remember the power of repeated readings of the same text for multiple purposes in keeping the interest of better readers, increasing strategy application by typical readers, and improving fluency of the poorer readers.

Guided Reading is taught with the recognition that a single text, reading method, and reading purpose on any given day does not mean that all children will achieve the same level of understanding. Guided Reading is also taught knowing that three other Blocks are providing rich and varied learning opportunities that support overall literacy development.

Guided Reading

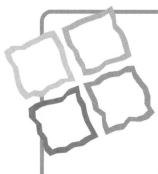

Purposes of the Guided Reading Block

The purposes of Guided Reading are to:

- help students develop the skills and understandings necessary to be strategic in reading a wide variety of texts

- provide experience in a wide variety of text types

- increase student ability to self-select and apply purposes for comprehending

How This Block Matters to Children with Disabilities

The Guided Reading Block is just as important for children with disabilities as it is for their classmates. Without instruction aimed at making meaning from text, children are left with an impression that reading is merely decoding words and successfully saying them aloud. This is a particularly important issue for children with disabilities, who often receive special or remedial instruction with too much focus on phonics and word reading and little or no focus on text comprehension. While word reading difficulties may contribute to a child's overall reading difficulty, addressing only word reading will not promote successful silent reading comprehension.

The ability to comprehend language has a significant influence on a learner's ability to comprehend written text. Many children with and without identified disabilities have language comprehension difficulties that impede comprehension. Some of these children have the label of language impairment, but others have labels such as autism, learning disability, or intellectual disability. Whatever the label, these children find it difficult to respond to comprehension questions or complete comprehension tasks, even when text is read aloud to them.

Some children have other types of disabilities that make comprehension difficult. For example, children with cerebral palsy and other neuromotor disorders may have difficulty reading words in sentences and paragraphs, even though they can read those same words presented one at a time. This may be due to difficulties in moving their eyes across the words in text or difficulties interpreting the information they take in visually (i.e., visual perception rather than just acuity). Difficulties in reading connected text may also be the result of speech production issues that impede reading aloud. Beginning readers, who do not read aloud, can't take advantage of their listening abilities to support their comprehension. It doesn't mean they can't learn, it simply means they require more opportunities for good instruction and explicit support learning from their teachers to use their inner speech to support their reading. Children with language impairments, by the very the nature of their disabilities, require Guided Reading instruction that makes explicit the processes and strategies of reading and understanding text.

Children with Disabilities: Reading and Writing the Four-Blocks® Way • CD-104235 • © Carson-Dellosa

Guided Reading

In our work with a large school system, we have followed the reading development of a large group of students with identified disabilities across a number of years. Part of our work with the school system involves teaching the professional staff how best to determine the instructional needs of each child. In one school year, these diagnostic efforts revealed that 52 percent of the students with identified disabilities in the school system struggled with reading because of language comprehension difficulties. In contrast, 32 percent had word identification difficulties as the base of their reading difficulties.

Selecting the Texts to Use During Guided Reading

One of the important goals of Guided Reading is teaching children how to read and comprehend many different types of text. In addition to the five text types that are commonly included in Guided Reading instruction (fiction, nonfiction, plays, poetry, and directions), teachers with children who have disabilities should select texts that represent a variety of media. Books, newspapers, magazines, and other traditional text sources should be supplemented with a variety of forms of electronic texts including multimedia software and Internet-based materials. While experience with these sources is becoming increasingly important for all children, it is particularly important for children with some disabilities (for example, cognitive or physical impairments), who may require electronic text in order to read independently. If such text types are not a regular part of these students' Guided Reading experiences, they may find it difficult to read and understand such materials on their own.

Electronic texts can be acquired and produced in many ways as described in detail on pages 50–52. As a reminder, the most accessible electronic texts are available on the Internet. The Internet Public Library (*http://www.ipl.org*) is one gateway to texts for young children. It also provides links to a variety of other sites on the Internet, including the largest available collection of public-domain antique children's books at (*http://www.childrensbooksonline.org*). Lyrics (and music) for hundreds of popular children's songs can be found at Kididdles (*http://www.kididdles.com*).

We also remind you that multimedia texts are available commercially in storybook (for example, Living Books® Library by Riverdeep) and nonfiction (for example, Start-to-Finish Literacy Starters and Readers by Don Johnston) forms. In addition, multimedia texts can be created by children and teachers using authoring tools that often are a part of the general education curricula (for example, KidPix® Studio Deluxe, AppleWorks®, PowerPoint®, etc.). Additional multimedia authoring software such as IntelliPics® Studio and My Own Bookshelf®, are more typically found in special education classrooms but are equally useful in inclusive classrooms, where students and teachers share in the responsibility for creating new texts to add to the classroom library.

Children with Disabilities: Reading and Writing the Four-Blocks® Way • CD-104235 • © Carson-Dellosa

Guided Reading

Before Children Read, the Teacher Helps Them

The Teacher's Guide to the Four Blocks® (Cunningham, Hall, and Sigmon, 1999) identifies several ways that teachers help children before they read text. These include:

- building and accessing prior knowledge

- making connections to personal experience

- developing vocabulary essential for comprehension

- taking a picture walk

- making predictions

- setting purposes

- starting a graphic organizer

- exploring text structure

Before-reading activities help children call upon appropriate prior knowledge or learn relevant background knowledge essential to reading text with understanding. The goal is not to teach the content of the specific text, but to ensure that students either have recalled or learned enough information to anchor what they will learn from reading.

Building and Accessing Prior Knowledge

In order to read with comprehension, it is necessary that a reader has sufficient background knowledge relevant to the text. While it can be overwhelming to consider all of the background knowledge required to understand a text completely, the goal on any individual lesson is to address the background required to complete the specific comprehension purpose or task that day. On subsequent days, new purposes and tasks will require additional background building. Across repeated readings for multiple purposes, children develop the broad background knowledge that may have appeared daunting initially.

Many children with disabilities have impairments that directly or indirectly influence their prior knowledge. For example, children with language, learning, and cognitive impairments may have limited prior knowledge due to their difficulties processing the information they have received throughout their lives. Often children with these disabilities have difficulties recalling personal experiences or understandings relevant to a particular text or task. They may find it difficult to make connections between different experiences (i.e., to see "the big picture"). They may find it challenging to understand that abstract text and two-dimensional pictures represent real life, or they may over-rely on real life experiences and background knowledge with little consideration of the specific text.

Children with Disabilities: Reading and Writing the Four-Blocks® Way • CD-104235 • © Carson-Dellosa

Guided Reading

Other children have disabilities that indirectly impair their abilities to acquire the breadth and depth of background knowledge that successful comprehension requires. For example, children with sensory, physical, and communication impairments have limited abilities to access information that children without disabilities experience daily. Children with sensory impairments may have been unable to casually listen to or observe others. Children with significant communication impairments may have been unable to ask questions about their experiences and children with physical impairments may have been unable to actively explore their environment. Children who have two or more of these differences are clearly at a disadvantage in terms of their ability to acquire world knowledge.

Teachers who have children with disabilities must engage in thorough background knowledge preparation, if they are to successfully engage students in guided reading. One efficient way that teachers both activate and assess background knowledge is to select core concepts and ask children to brainstorm what they know. For example, prior to reading *Tough Boris* by Mem Fox (Voyager Books, 1998), one first-grade teacher asked her class to list all of the things they knew about pirates and pets. The list and ensuing conversation helped the children recall what they knew about these topics and prepare to connect that knowledge to the book they were about to read. When a child with the label of autism offered what appeared to be unrelated information (i.e., lions, tigers, and elephants), the teacher responded by asking, "What makes you think of those animals?" When the child could not provide an answer, his classmates were eager to offer insightful connections, such as, "Eric, did you go to the Rainforest Cafe® and see that pirate with the lions, tigers, and elephants? I saw all of them when I went there for my birthday." The conversations that followed honored Eric's contribution and certainly helped him and all of the other students make connections with their prior knowledge related to pirates and pets. It was less important to know with certainty that the classmate had accurately identified Eric's intent and more important that the classmate found a way to link Eric's experience to the text they were about to read.

Children with language, learning, and communication impairments may have a difficult time with this kind of pre-reading vocabulary activity. Even if they have relevant prior knowledge, they may have difficulty recalling the words they know that correspond with that experience, or, as is the case with primary grade children who have significant communication impairments, they may not have a means to communicate what they know or remember.

An alternative means to assess prior knowledge would involve the use of pictures. The teacher gathers a set of pictures using an Internet photo search tool, such as Altavista (*http://www. altavista.com/image*). She prints or displays the images on the computer screen and asks the children to indicate which of the pictures are related to pirates and pets. In the current example, the teacher might have pictures of many kinds of pets, the ocean, boats, treasure, swords, maps, and other items that are related and unrelated to pirates or pets. As she shows the pictures to the children, they decide, individually or collectively, if the pictures belong in the columns labeled Pets, Pirates, or Others. Children indicate by pointing, responding yes or no, or by other means where a particular picture belongs.

Guided Reading

Once the teacher has a sense of the child(ren)'s prior knowledge, it is easier to make decisions about the prior knowledge that is necessary to teach. The most effective means of building prior knowledge is through direct experience of some sort. Watching a video, looking at pictures, having a conversation, and a variety of other means, can also develop prior knowledge. Today, teachers have access to thousands of short video clips on the Internet. In a few minutes, a teacher can search for videos on a given topic using search engines like Altavista *(http://www. altavista.com/video)*. Ultimately, the method of building background that is best suited to a given situation will be determined by the availability of time and resources. In the case of *Tough Boris*, it is unlikely that most classes would take a field trip to a pirate ship. They could, however, watch a clip from *Peter Pan* (available for free on the Internet), look at an information text about pirates, or talk with each other about pets they love and perhaps have lost.

Making Connections to Personal Experience

An important component of activating or building prior knowledge is helping children connect the current topic to personal experience. For children with the most significant disabilities, this often requires involvement from the child's family. If the child has difficulty recalling past experiences, finding the vocabulary to explain them, or simply does not have a conventional means of communication, the family must provide the information about the child's experiences.

Teachers make a habit of sending home a weekly note informing parents of upcoming texts and asking the parents to write a brief note about any experiences they have had with their children that might relate to the topic. When appropriate, parents might send in photographs or other materials that represent their children's experiences. Parents can also be encouraged to help children figure out how to communicate about their prior experiences. A less specific, but equally useful, approach would be to have a scrapbook at school that chronicles a child's experiences outside of school and in prior school years. The scrapbook can be added to on a regular basis with pictures and other records of experiences that can support both the memory of and communication about the personal experience. Children who cannot turn the pages independently can indicate through agreed signals when partners have found the right page and then use the same signaling system to identify the item on the page as partners point to each.

It is common practice to program the communication devices used by children with communication impairments with current, personal messages so that they can share their stories with others. These messages often convey funny, exciting, interesting, and personally meaningful information, and the messages are often reserved for use during unstructured interactions and scheduled sharing times. Unfortunately, the messages are often deleted after a week or two. For the purpose of supporting these communication device users in recalling and talking about their prior experiences, it is useful to organize and save these messages for use over the long term. Children who use light-tech systems or systems that won't store a nearly infinite amount of information might have old messages stored topically in three-ring binders. Messages in high-tech systems can be stored indefinitely but must be organized in an efficient manner if the child is going to find them later.

Children with Disabilities: Reading and Writing the Four-Blocks® Way • CD-104235 • © Carson-Dellosa

Guided Reading

Developing Vocabulary Essential for Comprehension

Within any given text, there is likely to be vocabulary that is unfamiliar to some children who will be reading it. Even the best vocabulary instruction cannot teach children all of the vocabulary they will encounter in text, but careful selection of vocabulary will support a child's ultimate success in comprehending the text.

As new vocabulary is introduced, be sure to help children connect it with existing vocabulary knowledge. Rather than teaching definitions that children memorize, use the words in contexts that are meaningful for the children and model use of the vocabulary. Support children in thinking of all of the words they know that relate to the new word being learned and discuss the ways in which the new word is like and unlike known words.

When children with significant communication or intellectual impairments are involved, it may be impossible to keep up with the pace of the new vocabulary that is being introduced. When this happens, be thoughtful about the vocabulary you chose to teach. Focus instruction on the words that appear more frequently throughout a child's life, not just words that are important in the current reading. For example, one boy we knew was engaged in a lesson that required him to know the word **escarpment**. A great deal of effort went into teaching him this infrequently occurring, specific word. Further, it was programmed on his communication device so that he could say it during class. It might have been more useful to help him see what vocabulary he already had available in his device to describe the concept, in this case "big, tall, hill, water." If he had described **escarpment** in this way rather than spoken the word, his teacher would have known that he understood the term. He also would have been able to incorporate this new word into his existing receptive vocabulary without complicating the use of his communication system with a new word that he would seldom use.

Another way teachers support students in making connections between new and existing vocabulary is to ask children to call out all of the words they can think of that are related to a target word. They encourage children to think broadly. For example, a child with learning and language impairments we worked with had a particularly difficult time linking new vocabulary to existing vocabulary. He was able to memorize definitions, but he seldom used the words. Instead of focusing on definitions, his teacher began to engage the class in this word-chaining activity.

On the first day of their desert curriculum unit, the teacher wrote new vocabulary on the board, including **desert** and **cactus**. The teacher asked the children to think of all the words they could that related to those two words. The children came up with obvious words like **place** and **plant**, but also **Wile E. Coyote**, **slivers**, and **mall**. The teacher asked the children who shared these less obvious terms to explain the connections. The first student explained, "When I think of the desert, I think of the Road Runner cartoon, which makes me think of Wile E. Coyote and all of the times he gets stuck by a cactus or does other things in the desert." The second student said, "I was thinking of those prickly thorns on the cactus. They made me think of the time I got a sliver in my hand, and my mom had to pull it out with tweezers." The third student replied, "The restaurant in the food court at the mall has all these decorations that make it look like a desert. They have this fake cactus there, too."

Children with Disabilities: Reading and Writing the Four-Blocks® Way • CD-104235 • © Carson-Dellosa

Guided Reading

Setting Purposes

An important part of all reading instruction involves helping children achieve cognitive clarity. In other words, we need to make sure students have a clear understanding of why they are doing what they've been asked to do, what they should be learning, and why it matters. Setting a clear purpose prior to reading supports students in developing cognitive clarity. Additionally, it focuses students and supports them in applying new strategies or applying old strategies in new ways.

As teachers begin to set purposes prior to reading, they find it helpful to use the words, "read this so that you can . . . ." This wording helps teachers monitor their own teaching and ensure that they are being very clear in setting a purpose for the students. It also gives students with disabilities the words they need to tell the teacher, "I am reading so that I can . . . ."

Graphic Organizers

Creating graphic organizers before reading allows students to understand how they might organize the understandings they develop while reading. For many children with disabilities the visual representation of their existing knowledge supports their use of what they know when reading. If part of a graphic organizer is completed before they begin to read, students can refer to the visual representation of their background knowledge and add new information as they read or after they finish.

It is important to teach a variety of structures for graphic organizers so that children come to understand that it isn't a particular type of organizer but the process of organizing information that supports their comprehension. We often find students misapplying a story structure organizer to nonfiction texts when they haven't been taught a variety of organizers and how to select the one that is appropriate for a given text.

There are also a growing number of technologies that can support students in learning and using graphic organizers independently. Kidspiration® (by Inspiration) is a software tool that supports semantic webs as well as linear and hierarchical graphic organizers. The advantage of Kidspiration® is that it includes text-to-speech so that the computer reads aloud the menu items and the words that are typed. Other graphic organizers include Inspiration (the grown-up version of Kidspiration®) and Draft:Builder® (Don Johnston, Inc.). When selecting a graphic organizer, consider how much structure you want to provide the children. The tools that offer the most structure tend to offer the least flexibility in creating various types of graphic organizers. Children who have difficulty following multiple-step directions and generating ideas often do better with a more structured graphic organizer technology. In contrast, children who have many ideas but lack the ability to organize them or put them together in a way that they can be communicated clearly to others tend to do better with more flexible graphic organizers.

Children with Disabilities: Reading and Writing the Four-Blocks® Way • CD-104235 • © Carson-Dellosa

Guided Reading

Variations During Reading

Actual reading should occupy the majority of a Guided Reading lesson. If children are going to improve their skill and learn new strategies for reading with comprehension, they must read! We often find that children with disabilities, because of their reading difficulties, participate in this portion of Guided Reading lessons only by listening. While the comprehension strategies being taught and the purposes that have been set are applicable in both reading and listening comprehension, children won't improve their silent reading with comprehension unless they have regular opportunities to read to themselves. Instead of resorting to listening when a text is too difficult for a child, consider alternatives to reading the complete text. For example, in the classroom at the beginning of this text, Linda spent most of the time listening, but she read the word **spider** whenever it appeared in the text. This alternative prompted her to look at all of the words in the text while her partner was reading so that she could identify the word she was able to read. Over time, that attention to the text, in addition to the other reading instruction Linda receives, promotes more text reading than does a listening structure.

One strategy we see overapplied in trying to support students with disabilities in their efforts to read independently is the use of symbols to support each word in the text. Similar to the use of rebus symbols to support students in reading one or two unfamiliar words in a new text, there is now software that makes it easy to type an entire book, and, with a single click, add a symbol to represent each word of the text. While there might be times when it makes sense to use this software to support students in accessing new content or a few difficult, unfamiliar words, using these symbol systems to represent all of the words in the text makes it even more challenging for the child to learn to read the words. More than two decades of research demonstrate that this practice diverts the reader's attention from the text. Reducing attention to the words obviously will have a negative influence on progress in learning to read and spell.

Some of the variations described in *The Teacher's Guide to the Four Blocks®* can be modified slightly to better support children with disabilities who read at levels significantly below their peers. These variations and some modifications are described below.

Choral Reading

All of the children read the text at the same time in choral reading. This helps children who can read most of the text and seems to work best with short texts, poetry, refrains, and books with a lot of dialogue or conversation.

Children who read at a level significantly below their peers can participate in this variation by reading a split second behind their peers. The directions need to be quite clear, however, that the children are to follow along in the text as they participate in this activity. The teacher might also select books for choral reading that have some pages of text that are easier than others. Some children can read all of these pages while others are only expected to participate in choral reading of the easier pages.

Choral reading is not appropriate for all children. For example, it is not appropriate to program whole words, sentences, or pages into communication devices so that children with

Guided Reading

communication impairments participate by pressing a single switch or activating a single button to match some portion of the text. This word-by-word matching (or picture-to-word matching) inhibits the fluent reading that these during-reading strategies are intended to support. If the child is expected to read each word and then say each word (or sentence or page) using the device, there is no chance for the child to develop an internal sense of prosody (intonation and expression) while reading or to develop the automaticity in word identification that is required for successful silent reading with comprehension. Instead of trying to create a way for these students to read aloud, encourage them to read silently with the group, using "the voices in their heads." Your instructional follow-up activities will help you assess how successfully these students were reading and understanding.

Echo Reading

In this variation, the teacher or another trained adult reads a line and the child reads the line back. Students work to match the adult's emphasis and fluency. This variation works best when the text has relatively short sentences and uses different voices.

Children can benefit greatly from hearing and copying the model of good reading provided in echo reading. Teachers might provide additional opportunities to children with disabilities to engage in echo reading by using either basic or computer technologies. For example, a teacher can record herself reading a short passage one sentence at a time, with a pause between each sentence that the child can use to echo what was read. Several children can listen and echo together as a means of preview before the text is read with the whole class or as a means of repetition with variety after the class has read the text.

Computer technology, especially talking word processors, can provide some support for echo reading, but it is difficult to get the speech synthesizers to read with the expression that readers rely upon to support their comprehension. When it is possible to record human speech and support children in listening to a digitized recording of human speech on the computer, the strategy is much more effective. PowerPoint® (Microsoft, Inc.) is a commonly available software product that would allow a teacher to type a single sentence on a slide and record her own voice reading the sentence. Children can see the text, hear it read, and echo read it before advancing to the next slide.

Shared Reading

As children and the teacher share in repeated readings of a book, the teacher gradually gives the children more and more control over the reading. This variation works best with predictable books, and, when used with a whole group, requires the use of a big book, chart, or multiple copies of the text so that all of the children can see the print.

Most often, children with disabilities have great success with this approach. One way to support children with disabilities so that they might experience even greater success is to provide additional opportunities to share in reading the text with an adult. A copy of the text is sent home for the child to read with an adult or sibling. Children might also share in additional readings with related service providers or other adults at school. Many children with disabilities who struggle with reading see a speech-language pathologist (SLP) as part of their educational

Children with Disabilities: Reading and Writing the Four-Blocks® Way • CD-104235 • © Carson-Dellosa

Guided Reading

program. Most SLPs can create dozens of ways to work an additional chance to echo read a text into their therapy sessions.

Partner Reading

Children with disabilities are often the children who have the most difficulty reading the texts during Guided Reading. These children need to be carefully paired with supportive partners who read more of the text than they might in other partnerships, and, often, adults need to join these partners when they are first paired to help them learn to negotiate the reading task in meaningful and mutually beneficial ways.

On "take turn" days, children with disabilities may have just a few words that they read when it is their turn. Sometimes, the struggling reader will read the first two or three words on each page. Other times, he is given three or four words that he looks for while his partner reads and chimes in. Some partners read aloud with the struggling readers following a split second behind.

There are simple technologies that could support children with significant communication impairments in taking turns during these partner-reading sessions. For example, a one to four-message communication device, such as a BIGmack® (*http://www.ablenetinc.com*) or a Cheap Talk 4 (*http://www.enablingdevices.com*), could be programmed with the word(s) that a child is responsible for reading. Children with significant communication impairments can follow along as the partners read and then use the device to read the correct word(s) when it is their turn. The key is to make sure the child with communication impairments is actually reading along with the text and not just waiting for a prompt to activate the device.

On "ask question" days, the struggling reader may study the page silently while the partner reads silently. Then, the partners read together orally before generating their questions and moving on to the next page. It is important to ensure that the successful reader does not skip the opportunity to silently read the text.

Children with some types of disabilities find it difficult to generate and respond to questions. Some children can be supported with a simple list of possible question words (who, what, where, why, when, how). Other students may require a few question stems to support them in generating questions. For example, some question stems might include:

- Why did the . . . ?

- Where is . . . ?

- Who is the . . . ?

Children who are partners with children with disabilities should be given the freedom to work with the children as true partners rather than assuming the role of teacher. Teachers should carefully consider alternatives to partner reading when they know that a text is very difficult or that a child with disabilities could be successful given the skilled coaching of an adult.

Children with Disabilities: Reading and Writing the Four-Blocks® Way • CD-104235 • © Carson-Dellosa

Guided Reading

Coaching Groups: Small, Flexible Groups

In many schools where the Four-Blocks® Framework is being implemented, coaching groups become a primary means through which special education and related service providers work with children with disabilities. In these classrooms, teams plan schedules together to ensure that extra hands are available during Guided Reading. Instead of taking the children with disabilities down the hall for reading support, the specialists go into the classroom and work with small, flexible groups of children that regularly include the children who have individualized education plans calling for support in reading. These groups change daily and include children with and without disabilities (including those who excel as readers), but the children with disabilities who struggle the most are assigned to a group more frequently to receive the careful coaching of a skilled teacher.

All of the children participate in the whole-class, before- and after-reading lessons, but they work in different groups, individually, or with partners during reading. The coaching groups provide a perfect opportunity for specialists to teach the children with disabilities who are struggling to apply the strategies they are learning during the Working with Words Block to reading and understanding connected text. Coaching groups make it possible for teachers to have a single before- and after-reading lesson that is paired with different texts being read by children either independently, with partners, or in their coaching group as described in the Three-Ring Circus below.

Three-Ring Circus

In the Three-Ring Circus, some children are reading independently, some are reading with partners, and others are reading in a small group with a teacher or related service provider. In many of the schools where we have seen coaching groups implemented well, the classrooms regularly implement a Three-Ring Circus strategy. The strategy becomes necessary when there are special education teachers and related service providers who cannot coach a group every day. The Three-Ring Circus allows the teacher to continue with a coaching group while some children read with partners and others read independently.

Book Club Groups

Book club groups provide another important way to meet the needs of children with disabilities in a class. Teachers can carefully select the easiest books to ensure that they match the reading level of the children who struggle the most. They can also include more than one easy book in the selections to increase the likelihood that children who struggle the most will select one of the easiest books. In other words, there is no rule that the teacher must have one hard, one medium, and one easy book. In some classrooms, a teacher may find it useful to have two easy books and one medium book with no hard books at all. The children who are the highest achieving will still be able to work on the comprehension skills and strategies being taught, and the teacher has increased the likelihood that struggling readers will experience greater success in completing the instructional tasks.

Children with Disabilities: Reading and Writing the Four-Blocks® Way • CD-104235 • © Carson-Dellosa

Guided Reading

Everyone Read To

Setting a clear purpose for reading, as is done in Everyone Read To (ERT), is highly supportive for many children with disabilities. Without this type of direction, children with a variety of disabilities may find it very hard to focus their attention, identify important ideas, and remember critical information from text. A simple ERT statement prior to reading focuses a reader's attention and increases the likelihood of success with any given comprehension task. When teachers identify more than one important purpose for reading a text, they can use the same text on another day with a new ERT statement to guide children. Children should not be able to address the purpose embedded in an ERT statement prior to (re)reading a text. In other words, every time a teacher begins, "Everyone read to . . ." she should be motivating children to read, not asking them to do something they can accomplish without reading and understanding the text.

Sticky Note Reading

Asking children to use sticky notes to mark interesting, important, and confusing parts of text is an especially effective way to maintain attention, particularly for children who are listening to, rather than actively reading, the text. Some children with disabilities may need their teachers to provide them with notes that already have questions or comments written on them. These children then place the notes in the appropriate places in the text without having to write on them. Some children may use sticky notes to mark the words they CAN read in a text instead of the words they struggled to read.

Another way to use sticky notes during reading is to provide children with a few sticky notes that have simple sentences written on them. These sentences are summaries of short portions of the text (sentences or pages) written with words the child can read independently. While the children with disabilities listen to partners read, they are determining which of their sentences means the same thing as the words they just heard. The child with disabilities then sticks the simple sentences on the appropriate pages in the book and effectively creates a re-authored version of the book that is at an easier reading level. On subsequent reads, the child with disabilities can read the sticky note version, and the partner can read the standard text.

After Reading

Discussing the Text

Teachers must address the challenge of keeping after-reading discussions focused. It is too easy to allow after-reading discussions to extend well beyond the length of time it took to read the book. Furthermore, it is difficult to keep children focused on discussing the book and relevant personal experiences and knowledge when the discussion is not focused. One way to maintain the focus of the discussion is to remind children why they have been asked to read the text in the first place before beginning the discussion. Remind them that they can write about other connections or ideas during writing time or share them with their friends during other times.

For example in a discussion about the characteristics of cats, James offered what appeared to be an unrelated comment about his pet hamster, "My hamster has a wheel in his cage." In

Guided Reading

response the teacher said, "Can you tell me what made you think of your hamster?" James replied, "I don't have a cat at home. I have a hamster." The teacher directed the response by asking, "Can you tell us one characteristic of your hamster? Tell us something about the way he looks or acts." James replied, "He is fast!" The teacher then tied his comment back to the original purpose by asking the class, "Is fast a characteristic of a cat? Could a cat be fast?" In the ensuing discussion, the class confirmed that some cats could be fast and several other characteristics of cats were shared. Particularly when children are reluctant to share, all of their attempts should be honored and shaped to integrate them into to the conversation at hand.

Connecting New Knowledge to Known Information

Relating new information to known information is a challenge for many children with language-based disabilities. These children often experience success with the new information in the context of the instruction, but have a difficult time generalizing the information to new settings, or storing the information for later recall.

Teachers can support students who experience these difficulties by explicitly teaching children to relate new to known information. Graphic organizers, described previously, are one method that provides a visual image of the relationship between new and known information. Teachers also find that they can support these students by carefully selecting books that share a theme. As the class progresses from one book to the next, teachers explicitly point out the connections between the books—relating new information in one book to the known information from the previous book(s).

In one classroom, a teacher systematically supported these connections across the entire school year. One wall of her classroom was devoted to a growing web that was created with small, white paper plates and yarn. As children read new texts or learned new information, they would literally connect it to their existing knowledge by writing about it on one of the plates and using yarn to connect it to their existing information. By the end of the year, the students had a sophisticated visual representation of the many connections between the books they had read together and the new information they had learned. More importantly, they understood the connections because they helped create them.

Predictions

Through the years, we have found making predictions to be particularly important when teaching reluctant readers. In our experience, reluctant readers are often older children who have experienced failure in previous attempts to learn to read. Consequently, they are reluctant to take risks as readers. Using a structured prediction format, such as a Directed Reading Thinking Activity (DRTA, Stauffer, 1969), is one way that we have successfully re-engaged these learners in reading for meaning. The DRTA begins with a brief preview of the first few pages of the text. The children are then asked to make predictions regarding what they think they will learn or what they think the book is about. Anything goes at this point. No value judgments are made regarding the predictions. They are simply written down, and children read to a predetermined, natural stopping point in the text. Then, children are encouraged to use what they have learned to revise existing predictions or make new ones. Again, no value

Children with Disabilities: Reading and Writing the Four-Blocks® Way • CD-104235 • © Carson-Dellosa

Guided Reading

judgments are made regarding the predictions; they are written down. Children continue reading to the end of the selection. Then, they discuss their predictions and how well they match what was actually learned or what actually happened. During this discussion, the children refer to the text to support their point of view.

Acting Out the Story

There are elaborate and simple ways to act out stories. While we value theater and all that students learn when they memorize lines, make or find costumes, and construct sets, none of these outcomes reflect our primary goal in acting out stories in our Guided Reading lessons. Here our goal is to use acting out as a means to support comprehension of the story. We find that we can meet our goal of supporting comprehension through very simple attempts to act out stories. Students can wear name tags or signs that indicate their roles instead of costumes or masks. They can use craft sticks with name tags instead of puppets. Texts can be used as a reference while acting out the story instead of memorizing lines. Narrators might tell the story while other children act it out, or children can act silently. There are a number of ways that all children can participate in acting out a story, but remember the goal—supporting comprehension of the story.

K-W-L Charts

K-W-L charts (Ogle, 1986) have long been used by teachers as an effective way to help children access prior knowledge and make predictions when reading informational text. This strategy is particularly effective when our lessons involve students with disabilities. Teachers use the same three-column format to guide children to identify what they know about a topic (K), what they want to know (W), and what they have learned (L). Because each component of the lesson is child centered, even children with severe disabilities are able to contribute at their own level of understanding. As classmates contribute what they know about the topic, children with intellectual disabilities build background knowledge and become aware of what they know that will be useful to the activity. The written K-W-L record provides a reference point for children with attentional, learning, or intellectual disabilities. Multiple contributions by different classmates increase the opportunities for children with intellectual or learning disabilities to make sense of key concepts and vocabulary in terms that they can understand. Teachers often turn copies of the K-W-L charts into personal books for the students with disabilities.

Graphic Organizers

Teachers who have children with disabilities in their classrooms know firsthand how effective visual representations of information can be for supporting memory, understanding, and communication. Many teachers rely on Inspiration® or Kidspiration® because these softwares allow them to create graphic organizers easily, modify quickly and repeatedly, turn the diagrams into outlines at the click of a button for writing, and to personalize supports for discussion and understanding with pictures and Web links. Some teachers will work with a small, mixed-ability group at a computer station to complete a Venn diagram, K-W-L chart, or one of the many other templates (for example, character webs, book comparisons, concept maps) available in the software. Other teachers have particular graphic organizers that they find useful to their

Guided Reading

classes, and they create their own templates for repeated use. Some teachers will import pictures or photos from the Web to further support student understanding, while others create Web links to sites that will enrich children's conceptual understanding. Many teachers will convert the web into an outline with a single click, then copy and paste the outline into a word processor for student note taking or other writing.

Writing Connected to Reading

For many children with disabilities, writing is the road to reading. Connecting writing to reading allows these children to experience more immediate success in comprehending what they read. There are a number of ways to connect writing to reading. For example, students can be told to read to a predetermined stopping place in a story. When everyone has read to the designated spot, they are then asked to write the ending to the story. Some students will only be able to write a few words, but they can work with partners who expand those few words into complete sentences.

Another way to connect writing to reading involves asking students to write what they would do or say if they were the main character in the story faced with a similar problem, or write a resolution to the story conflict, or write a portion of the story with new characters or in a different setting. Each of these can be done before or after children have read the story.

Making the Guided Reading Block Multilevel

We are often asked about including children with the most severe disabilities in Guided Reading lessons. The concern is what to do with a student who has severe mental retardation, no formal communication system, and no apparent ability to read. We think you teach that student.

Look at the book *Tough Boris* by Mem Fox (Voyager Books, 1998), for example. It is a story about a pirate who at first appears to be mean but turns out to be tender in the end. Mem Fox uses much more sophisticated language to describe Boris and has written a book that lends itself well to purposes for reading that focus on describing a main character.

The child with the most severe disabilities can participate in this discussion of Boris with as few as two communication symbols if the adults who work with the child can't interpret the child's attempts to communicate when more than two choices are provided. The two choices could be **happy** and **sad**. Words can be supported with picture symbols, gestures, or vocalizations. In building background knowledge, the child who is learning symbols can look at a symbol to direct his classmates to act it out. The teacher might say, "Tom is showing us the word happy. How do we usually let people know we're happy?" The other children respond by smiling broadly and laughing. Tom might even be able to participate in this acting out. The teacher could ask children to list activities or events that make them happy or sad, or the teacher could present children with a list of events and activities and then guide them in sorting the list based on whether the events would make someone happy or sad. Alternatively, the child with significant disabilities could practice selecting the words **happy** and **sad**. With each selection, the other children could be directed to write an event or activity that would make someone happy or sad.

Guided Reading

Children with Disabilities: Reading and Writing the Four-Blocks® Way • CD-104235 • © Carson-Dellosa

The teacher can expand the discussion beyond these two words to get the other children thinking, talking, and sharing their understanding of the way people's words, actions, and expressions help us to understand how they are feeling. For example, children could be asked to think of all of the other words that mean the same thing as **happy** and **sad**. Then, the teacher might introduce the book and tell children that they are going to read so that they can "talk about the way that Boris was feeling at the end of the book and why." Children could read in any of the formats discussed previously.

After reading, the group would get back together, and Tom could be asked, "Tom, tell us how Boris was feeling at the end of the story." Tom could provide a correct response (sad) and the group could go on to describe how they knew he was sad and discuss why they thought he was sad. If Tom gave the unexpected response (happy), the teacher can build on the response and use it as the basis of the ensuing conversation. For example, the teacher might say, "Tom thinks he is happy. Can anyone think of a reason why Tom might think Boris was happy at the end of the book?" Now the other children are stretched to think from a different perspective. As children attempt to take on Tom's perspective and explain why he may have thought Boris was happy (for example, "He made a new friend."), the teacher can guide them in looking back to the book for clues. After students have had an opportunity to probe this response, the teacher might ask, "Tom could have said that he thought Boris was sad. Is there anyone who thinks Boris might have been feeling sad? Why?" This could lead to acting out the story with an emphasis on the events that may have led to Boris's happiness or sadness (depending on the students' opinions) at the end of the story.

Summary of the Guided Reading Block

The purposes of this Block are to develop the language comprehension skills required to read and understand text. Teachers set clear purposes for reading, beginning each Guided Reading session with a before-reading activity aimed at building or activating background knowledge. They assist children during reading to independently read text to the greatest extent possible. They carefully plan after-reading activities and discussions that help children demonstrate the successful achievement of the purpose.

A Typical Week in the Guided Reading Block

A typical week in Guided Reading requires two texts, one at the average reading level for the class, and one that is easier. The first text is read for three days and the second text is read for the other two days. There are many different reasons that teachers might select the two texts. In the following example, the two texts are related topically. Other possibilities include two texts by the same author, two reflecting a particular genre, or two that share important vocabulary. In classes where there are children with disabilities requiring computer supports, the texts are scanned and imported into a talking word processor or, particularly for picture books, into a multimedia program such as My Own Bookshelf (*http://www.softtouch.com*), IntelliPics® Studio (*http://www.intellitools.com*), or PowerPoint® (*http://www.microsoft.com*). These books are burned on read-only CDs that are stored with a single copy of the book. When

Guided Reading

a child in need of computer supports is assigned to read the book, the original copy of the book sits next to the computer while the accessible version is read from the CD.

Monday

Before Reading

The teacher gathers children around and shows them the front cover of the book, *Fireboat: The Heroic Adventures of the John J. Harvey* by Maira Kalman (Puffin, 2005). She asks children to look at the pictures on the first few pages and think about what the book might be about. She reminds them that when they make predictions, they should use not only what they know about the topic and but also what they see in the book. After showing the class the first three pages, she asks children to make their predictions, and she records them on chart paper at an easel. When children build on each other's predictions, she adds the new information in a different color marker.

After the children have made predictions, the teacher tells them that they are going to read to the paper clip she's placed in each book and then check the predictions against the new information. She reminds them that they are going to write down the prediction they think is best, adding to others if needed, and then continue reading to the end before coming back together as a group.

The teacher hands out five copies of the book to five pairs of students. One of the pairs includes a child whose physical impairments make it impossible for her to hold a book and turn the pages. She and her partner take the copy of the book with CD and go to the computer to load the book. They open the book to the page with the paper clip so that they'll know when they've reached that page on the computer. As the pairs of children are moving to their reading spots, the teacher directs them to take turns reading. She then calls out the name of five children who are going to read with her and three more children who are going to read with the SLP.

During Reading

The class spends the next 15–20 minutes in their Three-Ring Circus reading the book. The teacher and SLP work with their groups using echo and choral reading to support the struggling readers. When their groups reach the paper clips, the adults work with the children to record what they think is the best prediction. They remind the students to look at the easel to see the predictions that everyone made before they started reading. All of the children write their predictions either generating a new one, selecting one from the list, or adding to one from the list.

The pair of students at the computer use a standard word processing program to record their predictions. The girl with physical disabilities uses an on-screen keyboard with a mouse to select the letters for the words she writes. Her partner uses the standard keyboard on the same computer to record his predictions.

After Reading

After all of the partners and groups finish reading the book, they return to the group to share their midbook predictions. The teacher asks the children to read their predictions and asks a

Children with Disabilities: Reading and Writing the Four-Blocks® Way • CD-104235 • © Carson-Dellosa

Guided Reading

few children to explain what information in the text led them to make their predictions. She leads the children in a discussion of the major story events thus far and their match with the predictions.

Tuesday

Before Reading

The teacher calls the group together and reminds them of the book, *Fireboat*, that they read yesterday. She asks the children to think of words they know that are descriptive. After getting a few examples, she asks the class to think about words they could use to describe people. As children begin to offer words, she records them in one of two columns: descriptive words and other words. Then, she tells the children that they are going to read today in order to decide which five words they think best describe the people who repaired and worked on the *John J. Harvey*.

The teacher again calls five pairs of children together and asks them to take turns reading. The child at the computer is joined by a new partner, who loads the CD to start up the book. She also calls the name of four children who will read with her and four children who will read with the special education teacher. She tells the children that they can write down the descriptive words they think are best while they are reading.

During Reading

The class spends the next 15–20 minutes in Three-Ring Circus reading. The teacher and the special educator use choral reading to support the struggling readers in their group. They make sure that they stop a few times while reading to suggest that students think about which of the descriptive words they think are best and to write some down to help them remember.

After Reading

When everyone has finished reading, the teacher calls the group together. She reads each word to the group and asks the children to look at the ceiling if the word is on their list. (The children look up instead of raising their hands because the girl with physical disabilities can't raise her hand but can look up.) Two of the children help her count and write the number of students who were looking up next to each word. When they've finished, the teacher underlines the five words with the highest number. She leads the children in a discussion of the five words. When one child suggests that the best word isn't one of the words with the highest number, the teacher asks the child to explain why he thinks a different word is the best word. The ensuing conversation provides an excellent opportunity for the class to look back at the book and discuss its characters.

Wednesday

Before Reading

The teacher begins reviewing the list of words made yesterday to describe the people who repaired and worked on the *John J. Harvey*. She shows the children a feature matrix she has drawn on the board. She explains that the children will use the feature matrix to describe the *John J. Harvey* by recording the types of equipment, the colors, and the uses of the boat.

Children with Disabilities: Reading and Writing the Four-Blocks® Way • CD-104235 • © Carson-Dellosa

Guided Reading

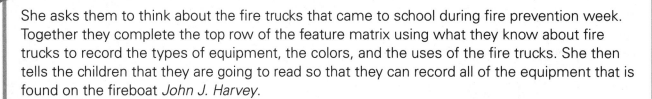

She asks them to think about the fire trucks that came to school during fire prevention week. Together they complete the top row of the feature matrix using what they know about fire trucks to record the types of equipment, the colors, and the uses of the fire trucks. She then tells the children that they are going to read so that they can record all of the equipment that is found on the fireboat *John J. Harvey*.

Today the teacher hands out nine copies of the book to nine pairs of children. She shows the children that she has tucked a copy of the feature matrix in the back of each book. She tells them to find a place where they can sit comfortably and both see the book because the whole group is going to read the book chorally today. As the children move into place, the teacher shows the girl at the computer and her partner the matrix they will use on the computer. (She left it open after she printed it for the other children this morning.)

During Reading
During reading, the teacher leads the class in choral reading. Half way through the book she stops, reminds children of the purpose, and asks them to turn and talk to their partners about the features of the *John J. Harvey* they've read about so far. After a few minutes, they continue reading to the end of the book.

After Reading
When the group has finished reading, the teacher asks the pairs to close their books and complete as much of the feature matrix as they can. She reminds them to try to complete the matrix first without looking back to the book. Finally, she pulls the group back together, and they work together with the book as reference to complete the feature matrix for the *John J. Harvey*.

Thursday

Before Reading
Today, the teacher introduces a new book, *Flying Firefighters* by Gary Hines (Clarion Books, 1993). She explains to the children this book is about a different kind of firefighting and asks them to look at the front cover and think about what that kind of firefighting might be. After a minute, she draws the now familiar K-W-L organizer on chart paper and asks children to tell her what they already know about flying firefighters. Once she has finished recording everything they know, she asks them what they want to learn about flying firefighters. She tells the children that today they are going to read in order to record two new things they learn about flying firefighters. Finally, she hands out 18 copies of the book. One of the children immediately goes over to the computer to load the CD for the girl who will read the electronic version of the book.

During Reading
During reading today, the teacher leads the group in reading the book chorally. They read the entire text beginning to end. The child at the computer reads "in her head."

Guided Reading

Children with Disabilities: Reading and Writing the Four-Blocks® Way • CD-104235 • © Carson-Dellosa

After Reading

The teacher asks the children to write down two things that they learned about flying firefighters. After the children have finished, she asks some of the children to read one of the things they learned aloud. When she has exhausted all of the new responses, she guides the children back into the book to find the places where they learned the new information.

Friday

Before Reading

The teacher begins by handing each student the feature matrix that was started earlier in the week and a copy of the book. She asks them to take a minute to look it over and remember the things they wrote about fire trucks and fireboats. They talk about the similarities and differences. Then, she tells them that today they are going to read to add one more row to their feature matrix. This row is going to be about flying firefighters.

During Reading

All but three of the children read the book silently today. The remaining three meet with the teacher at the small table and whisper read the book together.

After Reading

When all of the children have finished reading, the teacher reminds them that they should complete the feature matrix, trying first to fill in as much as possible without looking back at the book. After most of the children have finished, the teacher calls the group together and leads them through the book, completing the feature matrix as they discuss and look back at the book.

Children with Disabilities: Reading and Writing the Four-Blocks® Way • CD-104235 • © Carson-Dellosa

Guided Reading

Teacher's Checklist for the Guided Reading Block

In preparing and adapting my Guided Reading lessons to make them appropriate for the children with disabilities in my class, I have . . .

_____ 1. Selected at least one text each week that all children will be able to read independently after the last reading.

_____ 2. Carefully planned before-reading activities to teach key vocabulary and build or activate background.

_____ 3. Identified a clearly stated purpose for (re)reading the texts each day.

_____ 4. Created after-reading activities that allow students to demonstrate their successful reading for the given purpose.

_____ 5. Planned during-reading variations that ensure that struggling readers receive the required support while all students have maximum opportunities to read independently.

IEP Goals for the Guided Reading Block

Goals for the individualized education plan (IEP) in Guided Reading should reflect the skills and understandings that children are expected to learn as they engage in reading a wide variety of texts for multiple purposes. The overall purposes of the Guided Reading Block (page 64) include helping students develop the skills and understandings necessary to be strategic in reading a wide variety of texts and increasing student ability to self-select and apply purposes for comprehending. Here are some example goals for Guided Reading arranged from the lowest to the highest skill levels.

1. When engaged in a shared reading activity with an adult, the student will accurately identify and read 97 percent of the high-frequency words selected by the adult.

2. Given a passage at the <insert level one or more levels higher than current> reading level, the student will relate three or more newly acquired pieces of information to past understandings.

3. Given a narrative passage at the <insert level one or more levels higher than current> reading level, the student will make two or more predictions about the outcome of the story, read the story, and evaluate the predictions.

4. Given a narrative passage at the <insert level one or more levels higher than current> reading level, the student will summarize the story including information from the beginning, middle, and end.

5. Given a narrative passage at the <insert level one or more levels higher than current> reading level, the student will relate one or more story elements to his/her own life experience.

Guided Reading

Children with Disabilities: Reading and Writing the Four-Blocks® Way • CD-104235 • © Carson-Dellosa

the Writing Block is a powerful part of the Four-Blocks® Framework for many children with disabilities. Assistive technologies make it possible for children with a wide variety of disabilities to see, hear, produce, and process print more readily than ever before. Children can hear what they write as they type words into talking word processors. Children can bypass spelling difficulties or physical impairments by dictating a text to the computer or typing with word prediction software. Children who may be physically unable to paint or draw, can illustrate stories with graphic images they create, select, and modify in drawing software. Children with reading difficulties can read their own and classmates' writings with the support of digitized or synthesized computer speech. Children who have organizational difficulties can use webbing and outlining tools to explore and arrange their thoughts.

The Writing mini-lesson often involves the teacher modeling not only what writers **do**, but also what technologies writers can use to support success or increase independence. During the Writing Block, children write new drafts, assist each other in revising, edit self-selected pieces for publication, and augment their final drafts with various media and multimedia ranging from drawing and painting to digital images, movies, and online books with animated illustrations. Teachers meet individually with a few children each day, and children share drafts of recently completed work or work that is in progress.

Writing

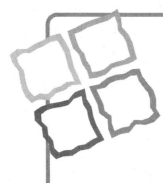

Purposes of the Writing Block

The purposes of Writing are to:

- help students develop the skills to independently write a wide variety texts for real purposes on topics of interest

- help students explore written language more slowly, personally, and carefully than the structure of reading activities allows

- provide opportunities for students to share their writing with peers and respond to others' writings

- provide opportunities for teachers to conference individually with children about the texts they are composing

How This Block Matters to Children with Disabilities

The Writing Block is vital to children with disabilities. Some children with disabilities learn to read by writing. Some learn to speak by writing. Some learn to think more clearly or solve problems more effectively by writing. Writing benefits children with disabilities by requiring them to attend closely to letters and letter/sound relationships. Writing slows down the process of message construction and enables children with disabilities to examine how ideas relate to each other.

The Writing Block is also vital to teachers of children with disabilities. When children write their names on sign-in sheets, make journal entries, contribute to language experience stories, or write with a word-processing program, teachers have the single best window into these students' understanding of print forms, content, and use.

A wide variety of technologies and curricular modifications enable teachers to support children's writing difficulties. The developing text itself serves as a reference point for children with attention difficulties. Assistive technologies support spelling, reduce or eliminate letter-by-letter typing, enable children to hear some or all of the text read aloud, adjust text size and color (as well as the background color of the screen), and organize their thoughts with pictures and diagrams.

One of the initial challenges for teachers is determining what combination of such supports will constitute a working "pencil" for each of our students with disabilities. However, because writing is inherently individualized (i.e., children can only write at their own level of understanding and skill), inclusion of children with disabilities is relatively easily achieved in this Block.

Children with Disabilities: Reading and Writing the Four-Blocks® Way • CD-104235 • © Carson-Dellosa

Writing

Mini-Lesson

A 10-minute mini-lesson begins each Writing Block. While we are tempted to allocate much more time to direct instruction, we have found that, in order to make sense of our instruction, children with disabilities need as much, if not more, time for writing as their peers without disabilities. Often they compose at slower rates, and always they need opportunities to apply what has been taught in the context of their own writing. In the mini-lesson, the teacher uses one or more of the students' writing tools as she models the thinking processes of composition. For example, she may type at a talking word processor, which feeds into a television monitor mounted high on the classroom wall where all of the students can see it. She models strategies such as brainstorming ideas or using the Word Wall. She types a few invented spellings so that children can hear the computer attempt to pronounce those combinations as real words only when vowels are included in the spelling attempt. The teacher frequently uses a fish bowl technique to help students learn how to provide each other writing feedback that is both helpful and respectful.

Children Writing and Teacher Conferencing

After the mini-lesson, children work on their own writing. Some compose together with a talking word processor. Others take earlier paper drafts from their writing folders to revise. Since children with disabilities vary widely in their abilities and independence, the teacher is careful to ensure that individuals, pairs of students, and small groups (and their technologies!) are all working smoothly before she begins conferencing individually with a few children each day. When the classroom has an aide or the child with disabilities has a one-to-one aide, the aide typically assists the student with disabilities in applying the mini-lesson strategy, process, or tool in that day's writing, but does not do so to the exclusion of opportunities for the child to interact with peers or conference with the teacher individually.

During the writing conferences, the teacher often helps the children with disabilities in learning a particular aspect of their "pencil," guides them in focusing on a single point of revision prior to publication, and explores possible writing topics and forms for future writings. Neither the teacher nor the other classroom assistants worry about nonconventions that have not yet been addressed in class; however, they correct them for children if they think the nonconventions will interfere with classmates' reading. The teacher has coached parents to respond to the content and not the form of writings the children take home. By sharing student writing samples from the fall, winter, and spring of her previous year's class, she shows parents the kind of growth they might expect in their own children's use of conventions this year as they gain fluency in all of the complex processes of writing.

Sharing

Author's Chair completes the Block. A few students read parts of drafts in progress. At times, an aide will help a child quickly import a draft into a multimedia program or talking word processor so that a nonspeaking child can read a text aloud, or a child with reading or writing difficulties is more willing to share drafts in progress. Often, one child's good idea gets

Writing

translated into multiple poems, stories, and other writing projects by other children in the class. The teacher is happy to see this active search for new forms and topics in her young students. All of the children's finished writings are published and added to the classroom collection in a wide variety of forms ranging from paper to multimedia CDs to online hypertexts. The teacher has found these many forms of publication motivating for students, more accessible to many families, and an inexpensive way to augment her classroom library.

Variations in the Writing Block for Children with Disabilities

The primary purposes of the Writing Block are to develop the skill and will of writing. Teachers assist children in gaining fluency in recording and revising their ideas and confidence in communicating those ideas to others. Children with disabilities often vary in educationally significant ways from classmates. Here are some examples.

Emergent Writing

Through grade 3, many children with disabilities, particularly those with severe or multiple disabilities, are emergent writers. Many of these same children also possess communication impairments that make it difficult for them to read aloud or interpret what they have written for others. This presents not only pragmatic, but also instructional difficulties in elementary classrooms, since teachers and classmates cannot provide feedback to nonconventional writings without accompanying oral interpretation.

Teachers employ a wide variety of strategies to reduce this uncertainty. Some teachers use experiences or pictures to prompt student writing. They find it easier to guess what a child means when writing **srks** if the accompanying picture shows a circus tent. On other occasions, teachers will engage a group of children in generating a structured language experience (Cunningham, 1979; McCracken and McCracken, 1986) in which a sentence frame is repeated. The children complete the frame with a particular category of information (for example, favorite foods or activities). For children who use picture symbols to communicate, some teachers will create a picture-based keyboard on Intellikeys® (Intellitools, Inc.). The keyboards may limit the word choice and creativity of young writers if used exclusively, but they also result in conventionally spelled texts that are more easily read by others, and they provide much-needed scaffolding for some children's severely delayed spelling or word order.

For children with spelling difficulties who have greater print experience, teachers often encourage the use of talking word processors. As the children hear the computer pronounce what they are typing, they are more likely to recognize and correct their own misspellings in order to get the computer to "say it right." On other occasions, teachers will use familiar experiences or familiar patterned storybooks to prompt writing on similar topics or with similar structures. When children write **F U GV DG CKE** patterned on the familiar storybook *If You Give a Mouse a Cookie* by Laura Joffe Numeroff (Laura Geringer, 1985), most teachers can decipher the child's "If you give a dog a cookie."

Children with Disabilities: Reading and Writing the Four-Blocks® Way • CD-104235 • © Carson-Dellosa

Writing

Many teachers also send home uninterpretable written products that are important to children. They send accompanying notes asking parents or siblings to try to negotiate the meaning with the student and send it back the next day. An unsuccessful, 15-minute guessing game about a nonspeaking child's favorite music, "B," was resolved in 30 seconds with a telephone call to the child's brother ("Beach Boys"). Communication, both face-to-face and written, is a continual negotiation process that is assisted by pictures, the environment, and familiarity of the reader or listener with the child who has disabilities.

The "Write" Stuff

We all have favorite conditions for writing. We like to sit in a particular location, to have a favorite beverage at hand or to listen to particular kinds of music. Some children with disabilities either will not or cannot write until we help discover what these conditions are for them. Here are some examples of children we've known.

Eric is a boy with autism. He would not engage in writing with a pencil or a keyboard or any other writing tools. One day he was given a labeler, available from any office supply store. He began writing by typing with this labeler, cutting off his message phrase by phrase, handing it to his one-to-one aide to peel the backing off, and then sticking the label onto his writing page.

Kyle was able to identify letters of the alphabet but did not write them with a pencil in a way that others could read. His teacher, while continuing to practice handwriting, introduced a keyboard, and Kyle immediately typed out his name and other words.

Josh wouldn't talk and was not believed to have any conventional literacy skills. However, when his kindergarten teacher brought letter stamps into the writing center, he selected the letters for his name and stamped it from left to right.

Brian could make barely legible letters with a pencil, and his spelling difficulties were severe. His teacher tried a keyboard and found that his written product was a little easier to read, but the spelling difficulties remained. She introduced him to a spelling prediction software, Co:Writer® (Don Johnston, Inc.), and found that Brian wrote faster in full phrases and sentences, and he used a wider variety of words. Suspecting that he knew more science and social studies than his second-grade writing revealed, she allowed him to give his answers to test questions orally. She discovered he knew as much content as anyone in the class when his writing tool didn't mask that knowledge.

Terry had severe physical impairments and typed very slowly with a keyboard equipped with a keyguard (for example, Turning Point Therapy and Technology, Inc.). He frequently appeared to type the letters of words out of order (**hnda** for **hand**, **cta** for **cat**, **fgor** for **frog**). The teacher wondered if these difficulties were spelling related or might result from the intensive physical effort that typing required of Terry. Working with a special educator, she replaced his keyboard typing with a joystick, an on-screen keyboard (now a free accessibility option in Windows operating systems), and Co:Writer®. Within a few weeks, Terry was typing more easily and spelling more accurately.

Writing

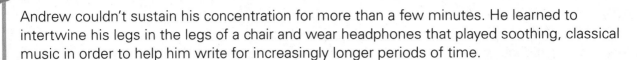

Andrew couldn't sustain his concentration for more than a few minutes. He learned to intertwine his legs in the legs of a chair and wear headphones that played soothing, classical music in order to help him write for increasingly longer periods of time.

Teachers, often working in collaboration with occupational therapists, special educators, speech-language pathologists, and parents, begin exploring appropriate pencils whenever writing seems labored, slow, or inaccurate for students. Children with fine motor difficulties often can write, but their handwriting is both difficult to read and slowly produced. Perceptive teachers continually seek out improved technologies and supports for reducing the physical and cognitive difficulties associated with writing so that children can focus on communicating meaning. This is particularly important for beginning writers who must juggle the cognitive, linguistic, communicative, and physical demands of writing all at the same time. Finding an alternative to a pencil or pen often eliminates the physical demands and allows the beginning writer to focus on the other three. If the child has the physical ability to be able to write with a standard pen or pencil one day, it is much more likely to occur when the child is motivated and able to write in order to communicate meaning.

Simple Adaptations

Pencil grips are familiar to most teachers and easily available from teacher supply stores. For some children with fine motor difficulties, these simple devices make a pencil easier to manipulate. Other children with more severe physical impairments can sometimes write by using a tennis ball with a pencil poked through it. They find it easier to grip the larger tennis ball than the slender pencil or smaller pencil grips. Still other children find it easier to write when their paper is taped to a slanted desktop.

Sometimes children don't want to write, even though they can. Rather than turning this reluctance or obstinance into a battle, or an exercise in rewards and punishments, teachers seek more motivating tools (and motivating instructional experiences!). One teacher used Duplo cars with markers hot glued to the end to get young boys writing by driving. Another teacher got some of his students writing by letting them sharpen their pencils in the nostril of his nose-shaped sharpener. Teachers stock their writing center with a wide and ever-changing array of pencil and paper variations including Magna-Doodle, portable chalkboards, miniature white boards, blank books, typewriters ("It's like a computer with paper," teachers explain.), magic markers, paintbrushes, crayons, fat pencils, skinny pencils, name pencils, and vibrating pens. One teacher motivates her students with a large container full of interesting pens she has collected in her travels: pens shaped like fish, ghosts, bones, snakes, birds, aliens, a wand for blowing bubbles, and more.

Most teachers discover as they begin this problem-solving process that there are many databases that help them efficiently explore writing tool options, including:

- **Closing the Gap's Resource Directory**
  (*http://www.closingthegap.com/home/about_rd.lasso*)

Writing

- **AbleData Database** (*http://www.waisman.wisc.edu/index.html*)
- **Family Village** (*http://www.familyvillage.wisc.edu/index.htmlx*)

Writing, Revising/Editing, and Publishing

It is critical for children who struggle in learning to read and write to get many repetitions with their writing tools across texts and tasks. Revision is one of the natural ways that repetition with variety is easily incorporated into writing instruction. Because children with disabilities often write slowly or with incomplete thoughts and invented spelling, or because their syntax is often unconventional, revision accomplishes a number of important instructional goals. It allows teachers to help children expand on their thoughts, explore their word choice, and practice the use of their writing technologies. It enables the teacher or aide to help the child express the intended message more conventionally and keeps the focus of that convention use squarely on communication.

Eric, a boy with autism, after viewing a picture of an injured bird, wrote:

BIRDS OWIE HERTS.

His aide worked with him the next day to revise the text, asking questions like: "How did the bird get hurt? What do you think will happen to the bird next? How do you think the boy who found him feels?"

Eric's revised text read:

BIRDS OWIE HERTS

ARROW IN THE BIRD

BOY IS SADE

XSNDINT

AMBULINS

Eric wrote another text for a subsequent picture that was very confusing to readers:

BIRD DINNER EATING BOY

His teacher, aide, and mother could not determine if he meant the boy and bird were eating dinner together, if the boy was eating the bird's dinner, if he was suggesting that the boy was the bird's dinner. After revision, his text read:

BIRD DINNER EATING BOY

BIRDS EATING WERMS

While this didn't clarify all the questions entirely, it suggested that he was writing about the boy eating dinner with the bird, who was eating worms.

Writing

Children with Disabilities: Reading and Writing the Four-Blocks® Way • CD-104235 • © Carson-Dellosa

Eric's aide understood several important ideas about beginning writing. First, she knew that if Eric were to invest in the writing process, she couldn't put her words in his mouth but rather had to help him find his own message. Consequently, she asked lots of open-ended questions. Second, she understood that revision for most beginning writers is simply addition of more ideas. She didn't demand reordering of the ideas before Eric was ready to work on word order himself. Third, she understood that editing and revision are two different processes and that if she was going to help Eric elaborate upon his thoughts, she couldn't interfere with spelling or grammar cleanups until later. She made notes for the teacher about conducting mini-lessons on word and sentence order, sentence expansion, and sentence combining. She made additional notes about the importance of working sequencing of ideas into the pre-reading activities and purpose-setting step of Guided Reading lessons for Eric.

Writing for Real Reasons

Because of their differences, children with disabilities often come to school with fewer, or different, experiences than nondisabled peers. They often have spent more time in hospitals and clinics and offices, less time playing outside or visiting friends' houses, less time exploring print or being read with. These differences mean that children with disabilities often experience difficulty in relating new learning to previous experiences and in generalizing from the particular instructional experience to its wider application.

For these reasons, we make sure that children are clear about why they are engaged in particular writing activities, we apply skills taught in mini-lessons immediately and repeatedly in children's text writing, and we write as often as possible for a wide variety of authentic audiences. For example, Michael was a young boy whose learning difficulties made it extremely difficult for him to spell conventionally. In a weekly spelling test, he had written multiplication this way: **M**. His teacher taught him the basics of Co:Writer® in a mini-lesson, including how to:

- open the program and link it to a word processor

- type a letter and search the suggested words for the one he was trying to spell

- place the mouse over a word to hear the computer speak it aloud if he was not sure how to read it

- use end punctuation (or ENTER) to transfer his sentence from Co:Writer® into his word processor

- use the +/= key to return to Co:Writer®

His aide suggested that Michael try to write **multiplication** by using Co:Writer®. Michael again typed **M**, and Co:Writer® produced **multiply** among the choices. Michael clicked on it, heard the pronunciation, selected it, deleted the **y**, and chose **multiplication** from the resulting list. Michael and his teacher immediately understood the importance and utility of his using Co:Writer® during writing activities.

Children with Disabilities: Reading and Writing the Four-Blocks®Way • CD-104235 • © Carson-Dellosa

Writing

Writing for real and immediate audiences is vital for young writers with disabilities. When peers in writing groups laugh at a funny story, connect with the pain of losing a pet, or ask questions about a favorite experience, they create motivating reasons to struggle with the difficulties of spelling, word choice, and grammar. Teachers continually seek real audiences for their students beyond the immediate classroom and school.

Several teachers we know have established relationships with teacher education programs. Pre-service teachers e-mail or snail mail with children in their classes. Pre-service teachers gain firsthand knowledge of the writing interests and skills of the children, and the children are excited to write to their new friends, especially when they live in different parts of the country. Several children with disabilities in Minnesota were unable to locate Iowa on a map, but they knew where their pen pals in North Carolina could be found; they worried about them when hurricanes blew through the state; and they celebrated with them when the Tar Heels won a basketball championship.

Other teachers have employed Instant Messenger during their computer lab time as a regular opportunity to write with pre-service teachers or partner classes in other parts of the country or world. Another teacher found that she could reduce the children's online spelling errors by opening Co:Writer® and linking it to Instant Messenger.

Some teachers are exploring online bulletin boards (for example, *www.nicenet.org*), chat rooms, blogs, and wikis as online environments where students can contribute to the learning of communities of various sorts (for example, people interested in a particular kind of music, people learning about another part of the world, people exploring geologic events, etc.).

Still other teachers take advantage of children's interests to show them immediately the importance and value of writing. They show them how to download pictures and short music or video files from the Internet (for example, Google image searches or Altavista media searches), insert them in word documents or HyperStudio stacks or KidPix slideshows, and then author texts about these cherished interests.

Writing

Supporting Author's Chair

Use of an Author's Chair enables teachers to develop a community of writers in the classroom and to support children's developing interests in writing as a form of communication and thinking. However, many children's individual differences make it difficult for them to share their writing with other students. Here are some difficulties you may encounter and some of the solutions that teachers have employed.

Bradford is a young boy with Down syndrome whose speech makes it difficult for others to understand him. He is aware of this difficulty and consequently painfully shy about speaking in front of the class, as Author's Chair requires. Previous experience had convinced the teacher that she could get all of the children to voluntarily share their writing by modeling positive feedback and constructive criticism ("I hope you'll tell us more about how you felt when you saw the snake. That's a really interesting and scary part of your story."). However, Bradford still was not volunteering to share almost eight weeks into the school year. Although Bradford could write with a pencil, the teacher decided to have him write one of his drafts at the word processor with Intellitalk (a talking word processor). The teacher allowed Bradford's friend to accompany Bradford to the computer during Author's Chair. Bradford had the computer read his writing aloud and beamed when the students told him how much they liked his poem.

Ronnie is a young boy with cerebral palsy. He is able to voluntarily control only his eye movements, and he composes by dictating to an aide. He looks at pictures, letters, words, and phrases mounted on a clear acrylic sheet called an eye-gaze frame. The aide sits facing him, interprets where he looks on the frame, and writes down the text for him. Ronnie takes a turn in the Author's Chair by selecting a classmate to come stand beside him and read his text aloud. Ronnie then answers classmates' questions by eye pointing to his board. The aide is training classmates how to interpret his eye pointing responses.

Carly is a young girl with significant multiple disabilities including visual and hearing impairments. She is learning to use two switches to direct her one-on-one aide during writing time. The aide has a communication notebook that includes pages with many words and symbols arranged in categories. Carly doesn't know all of the words and symbols in her notebook, but writing provides an excellent opportunity for her to learn them. The aide works with Carly to select a topic for writing from the topic page in her notebook. The aide uses a mini-flashlight to point to each of the options while she says them aloud. Carly directs the aide through the process by using one switch to tell the aide, "tell me the next one," and the other to say, "that's the one I want." The aide waits patiently while Carly decides which switch to hit and writes down all of the words that Carly selects from her notebook. When she's finished, the aide records what Carly has written onto one of the switches, and Carly can read aloud what she has written.

Children with Disabilities: Reading and Writing the Four-Blocks® Way • CD-104235 • © Carson-Dellosa

Writing

Multimedia Publication

Teachers in Four-Blocks classrooms including children with disabilities often opt for more frequent multimedia publication of children's writing. This is sometimes as simple as including a taped version of the author reading the text aloud. Some children, who can read independently, simply enjoy listening to their classmates reading aloud. Other children require the taped story support in order to read the story or particular words. Parent volunteers often coordinate the tape-recording process.

Other teachers teach their children to use a multimedia tool such as PowerPoint®, AppleWorks®, HyperStudio®, or KidPix® Studio Deluxe to author their books. Children enter text, Quicktime® movies, music files, and their own voices reading the text aloud. These texts often become the most widely read and discussed in the classroom. Beyond the creation of this additional publication outlet, teachers find that the young authors and readers in their classes expand their conceptual understanding and vocabulary in the process of creating these hypertexts. They also find that their students are motivated to engage in repeated readings of the text as they read, listen to themselves, and strive to get it "just right."

Still other teachers import children's texts into talking word processors (for example, WriteOut: Loud®) where children enjoy listening to the computer read their texts aloud. Teachers and children can change the computer voice reading the text aloud to maintain children's interest and attention while motivating repeated readings of the text.

A Variety of Mini-Lessons
What to Do When You Can't Spell a Word

Many children with disabilities experience significant and continuing difficulties in spelling. The Word Wall and other activities in the Working with Words Block are particularly important for such children. The strategy of spelling words the way they sound is also particularly important.

Additional technologies are also worth teaching children in order to support wide vocabulary use and greater independence in their writing. Children who have difficulty speaking, difficulty in processing spoken sounds, or who have severe physical impairments that make it difficult to hold a pencil or to type fluently often require additional tools or supports. Two technologies are particularly worthy of mini-lesson instruction and classroom follow-up. One is the use of a talking word processors, such as WriteOut:Loud® (Don Johnston, Inc.), IntelliTalk® II (IntelliTools, Inc.) or AppleWorks® (Apple Computer, Inc.). Teachers, special educators, speech-language pathologists, and others chose the appropriate talking word processor by carefully considering the features that are most important for the children they are trying to support. Some talking word processors literally read the letters and words in the document. Others include options for providing on-screen word and picture banks. Still others include sophisticated, talking spell checkers. Sometimes more is not better as some children (and teachers) get overwhelmed when there are too many features available. At the same time, there are children for whom simply reading the letters and words on the screen is not supportive enough.

Children with Disabilities: Reading and Writing the Four-Blocks® Way • CD-104235 • © Carson-Dellosa

Writing

For a mini-lesson focused on the use of a talking word processor, the teacher projects her computer on a television monitor or the school's LCD portable projection system. In some cases, the teacher might use the school's computer lab to teach this lesson. The goal is to ensure that all of the children can see as she launches the talking word processor program and sets the voice feedback at the letter and word level so that the class will hear each letter she types and each word as she writes and thinks aloud. She then proceeds with her mini-lesson typing on the computer and drawing the children's attention to the word processor as it speaks.

Co:Writer®

Another technology that is even more supportive for children with more severe spelling and syntax difficulties is word prediction software, such as Co:Writer® (Don Johnson, Inc.). When introducing the use of word prediction, teachers set up the software to provide five choices so that children have several words from which to choose but not so many choices that they are overwhelmed. (Co:Writer® can provide up to nine choices.) Teachers demonstrate using both the standard prediction and flexible spelling options. The software then uses word frequency, recency of use, grammatical accuracy, and developmental spelling patterns to guess at words being typed. The teacher demonstrates the use of this tool to her class by thinking aloud and using a projection system connected to her computer.

"Today, I am going to use Co:Writer® to help me spell while I'm writing my story. I want to write about the story we read yesterday, *Russ and the Almost Perfect Day* by Janet Rickert (Woodbine House, 2001). I think I'll write, 'I like the story we read about Russ.'"

She begins to type in Co:Writer®, **I**, and hits the space bar. Next she types **L** (the computer suggests **liked**, **like**, **looked**, **look**, **let**). "Oh, look. The computer is guessing what I want to write. Does anyone know any of these words?" Children suggest some of the words, and the teacher moves the mouse over each one in Co:Writer® so that students can hear the word spoken aloud and learn to use this feature in their own writing. As the mouse moves over **liked**, the teacher says, "That one sounds a lot like the word I want, but I want to write about how I feel right now. I want **like** not **liked**. Oh, there's the word I want, **like**." She moves the mouse over the word and clicks on it. **I like** now appears in the Co:Writer® window.

She now types **T**. **To**, **the**, **that**, **them**, and **their** appear in the Co:Writer® window. Again, she asks the children if they know these words. Again, she shows them how to move the mouse over each word to hear it read aloud by the computer. With the next word she may decide to point out to students that Co:Writer® won't let her write the wrong word or a word that wouldn't make sense. In doing so, she shows them how each of the choices it does provide make sense when used in a sentence beginning with the words she's already written. The process continues to the end of the sentence, where the teacher asks the class, "What do we need to put at the end of our sentence to show the reader we're done with our idea?"

"A period," several children call out. The teacher types a period, and Co:Writer® disappears and the sentence appears in the word processor window. The teacher shows the children how to press the +/= key to get a new Co:Writer® window to appear. Together they type the next sentence.

Children with Disabilities: Reading and Writing the Four-Blocks® Way • CD-104235 • © Carson-Dellosa

Writing

Children with Disabilities: Reading and Writing the Four-Blocks® Way • CD-104235 • © Carson-Dellosa

We recently worked with a school that was implementing Co:Writer® in all of its third-, fourth-, and fifth-grade classrooms. Devon reminded us of the power of Co:Writer® on the first day that it was introduced in a mini-lesson much like the one described above. A struggling, reluctant writer, Devon typically wrote very short, "safe" sentences that included only words he knew how to spell. The first thing he did with Co:Writer® was fill the screen with the longest words in every list that was generated when he typed the letters on the keyboard. He proudly typed a letter, moved his mouse over the words to hear them read, and selected one to enter into his word processing document. After several minutes of this exploration, the first sentence he wrote was, "The dog crawled into the limousine, and his owner followed." As consultants, we didn't know that Devon typically had a great deal of difficulty writing. We saw how he approached exploring Co:Writer® and noticed the sentence we wrote. Impressed, we asked him to share it with his peers and congratulated him on his expert use of Co:Writer®. After school, the teacher thanked us for calling on Devon and told us it was the first time she had seen him show such confidence in his writing. Six weeks later, we were back in Devon's class. We commented on his writing, and he reminded us, "I'm the Co:Writer® expert. Remember? That's why my writing is so good."

Vowel Rules

Teachers often color code vowels with red in Making Words and other spelling and phonics lessons. This color-coding helps beginning readers and writers learn that every English word has a vowel. Talking word processors can be used to teach or reinforce this understanding. For this purpose, teachers set WriteOut:Loud® to provide voice feedback each time a letter or word (defined by the computer as a group of letters, containing a vowel, with white space on both sides) is typed.

For this mini-lesson, the teacher gathers a mixed-ability group or the child who requires additional assistance at a computer with a talking word processor. She engages the child(ren) in a word sort or other spelling activity. If the child types **CT** for cat, the word processor will speak only the letter names (SEE TEE). The child, hearing this, and sometimes being additionally prompted as necessary, thinks, "Oops, SEE TEE isn't a word, I must have left out one of those red letters." If she enters a vowel, the word processor then will pronounce the new word, **cat** (KAT) or **cot** (COT) or **cut** (CUT). Teachers color code the vowels on the computer keyboard using see-through stick-on labels purchased at office supply stores.

More advanced writers can learn a more sophisticated vowel rule using a word prediction program like Co:Writer®. As children learn to use Co:Writer® and can move from a list of five or six word choices to a list of nine, a new vowel rule can be taught. In this case, children learn to go back and change the first vowel in their spelling attempt, if Co:Writer® has not predicted their word by the third letter. Given nine choices in the word list, almost every word spelled correctly to the third letter will appear in the list. Through the years, we've learned that children who are having difficulty spelling words with the correct vowels are often quite successful in narrowing down or eliminating a few options that they know aren't correct. When taught to try a different vowel, these students are often quite successful in spelling the word correctly enough for it to appear in the list on the second attempt.

Writing

Reciprocal Structured Response in Writing Groups

Reciprocal teaching (Palincsar and Brown, 1986) is a strategy typically used to help children construct meaning from text and monitor themselves while reading. Some teachers use a similar structure to lead children in providing feedback to each other at the end of the Writing Block in groups or Author's Chair. They model the process or provide a sequence of feedback stems to use in talking to classmates about their writing. For example:

- The thing I like best about your writing was . . .

- One thing I'd like to know more about is . . .

- One thing you might do to make your writing even better is . . .

Children with disabilities sometimes need more guidance in the process to keep the discussion more focused on content and less on spelling or surface errors. One teacher devoted four consecutive mini-lessons to four strategies (summarizing, questioning, clarifying, and predicting). On Friday, she then asked students in groups of five to take turns with each member's writing:

- summarizing (In my own words, this is about _____.)

- questioning (One question I had about your story was _____.)

- clarifying (One thing that is confusing to me is _____.)

- predicting reader response (I think the class will like _____.)

With the added instructional focus, the connection to a strategy that students were already familiar with from Guided Reading, and the response stems, the student groups seemed better able to focus more on ideas rather than editing issues in each other's writing. They were better able to support the struggling readers in each group by referring to the response stems and modeling examples for each other.

I Don't Know What to Write/I Don't Have Anything to Write

Some children struggle in getting started with any given day's writing for a variety of reasons including:

- inexperience in writing on topics of their own choosing

- learned helplessness and a strategy of waiting when anything is difficult until someone provides a solution

- learned fear from papers returned with all of the nonconventions circled and marked as errors

Children with Disabilities: Reading and Writing the Four-Blocks® Way • CD-104235 • © Carson-Dellosa

Writing

Children with Disabilities: Reading and Writing the Four-Blocks® Way • CD-104235 • © Carson-Dellosa

Modeled journaling is one way a classroom aide got Jordan started writing. Jordan, a boy with severe communication and physical disabilities, often sat for long periods of time during the class's journaling time. If and when he wrote during this time, he typically selected whole messages stored in his communication device. He might, for example, choose with a single keystroke:

I went to a softball game last night. Dad's the coach. His team won.

While this was an efficient way for Jordan to share important events with classmates, he was learning nothing from the experience about sequencing ideas, spelling unknown words by ear and eye, or juggling the many aspects of the writing process he needed to learn in order to communicate unique ideas.

One day, the aide started journal time by telling Jordan, "I have an idea for journaling today. To begin, I want you to tell me what you want to write about today." She then worked with Jordan as he selected adults as a topic for the day. His aide then wrote where Jordan could see her, and she read aloud as she wrote:

I know a nurse. Her name is Mrs. Smith. She works at the hospital. I like her.

She then read aloud again the entire text to Jordan, put it away, and told him, "I can't wait to see what you're going to write." Jordan wrote through a combination of letter-by-letter spelling, whole words, and whole phrases:

I no teacher. Her name is Lee. She works at my school. I like Lee.

Many teachers have successfully used nonrhyming poetry models to enable some children to begin to compose more coherent texts. Kenneth Koch, a published poet, developed the approach and wrote many books about helping a wide variety of novice writers find their voice and develop their writing interests and abilities. Our favorite for young children with disabilities is *Wishes, Lies, and Dreams* by Kenneth Koch (Harper Paperbacks, 2000). The repetition, structure, and simplicity of these models seem to free children with disabilities to concentrate more on what they want to say without the at-times overwhelming complication of how they want to say it.

One teacher used a model of this type to help Megan, a young girl with Down syndrome, write her first poem. While the rest of the class worked in pairs to brainstorm objects, locations, and experiences related to a favorite color, the teacher worked with Megan and a small, mixed-ability group. They handled, explored, and discussed a variety of yellow items: bananas, apples, Tums®, pencils, pot scrapers, Juicy Fruit® gum, mustard, and a dish towel.

Writing

After this brainstorming and exploration, the children wrote simple five-line poems in which each line started with the favorite color and described it with one of the five senses. Megan's resulting poem read:

Yellow tastes lke set apples.

Yellow sels like gam.

Yellow fels like prakle skrapr.

Yellow sunds like jekle kande.

Yellow likes like spisse mustard.

Another strategy we have seen several first- and second-grade teachers employ is Gimme 5. With younger readers, the teacher often generates a class list of items like: five things we like, five things that scare us, five things that are gross, five people we'd like to meet, five places we'd like to go, five things that make us angry, and so on. With more capable readers, the teacher often directs the children to generate their own individual lists, which are then kept in their writing folders for reference when topics don't readily come to mind.

Recently, we observed a teacher who asked the class what kinds of books they liked to read and what they wanted to learn more about in books. The list included: dinosaurs, horses, mysteries, Captain Underpants, basketball, snakes, and a variety of authors. The teacher posted the list and encouraged children who were stuck on any given day to write about something their classmates (i.e., their most immediate audience) wanted to read. Students found it very motivating both as authors and as readers anticipating a new publication of interest.

Sentence Combining

Children with many different disabilities (and many without) find it difficult to make the transition from the short, simple sentences to longer, more complex sentence structures. One way we support students in making this transition is through the use of sentence combining. Our goal is to teach simple ways to take two or more sentences and combine them into one sentence using **and** as well as a comma to accomplish the task. In our mini-lessons, we model sentence combining using two sentences that we've selected because they are like the sentences the children use in their own writing. Each time we show one way to combine two sentences, we ask the students to help think of at least one other way we could do it. Then, we give students a few sentences to combine on their own and share with others before they begin writing.

Writing

Children with Disabilities: Reading and Writing the Four-Blocks® Way • CD-104235 • © Carson-Dellosa

Making the Writing Block Multilevel

Writing, because text creation is slower and more meticulous than text reading, is critical to the literacy learning success of many children with disabilities. Children explore words letter by letter, investigate letter-sound relationships, and see the impact of their word choices on classmates and other readers. Our guiding principle (as with Cunningham, Hall, and Sigmon) in implementing the Writing Block is that children must select their own topics and forms in order to improve not only their writing skills, but also their interest in and use of writing beyond the classroom walls.

Rashon was a young second grader whose spelling and learning difficulties led to little text production and decreasing interest and effort in classroom writing. One day, his teacher noticed that he was engrossed in one of Dav Pilkey's *Captain Underpants* series (Blue Sky Press/Scholastic). She discussed the book with him, and seeing the sparkle in his eyes, suggested during Writing Block that he compose his own *Captain Underpants* comic. The resulting text read:

> Wedgie Man by Rashon
>
> one da y while wedgie Man was
> waching tv. He
> sawa commercial
>
> all on the sudden wedgie
> Man bumped into
> Dr. evil
>
> all of the sudden
> dr. Evil pushed
> The BUTTON
>
> Owho Toilet Droids
> wedgie man use d
> wedgie power
>
> Then He
> dropped dr. Evil in prison
>
> A Rashon Classic

Children with Disabilities: Reading and Writing the Four-Blocks® Way • CD-104235 • © Carson-Dellosa

W R I T I N G

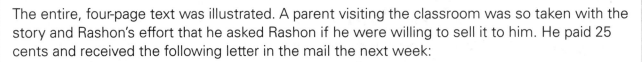

The entire, four-page text was illustrated. A parent visiting the classroom was so taken with the story and Rashon's effort that he asked Rashon if he were willing to sell it to him. He paid 25 cents and received the following letter in the mail the next week:

Thank you

For buying

My comic book

Rashon

Effective teachers of children with disabilities recognize that they cannot teach specific genres, or improve the form of children's writing, before children begin writing many texts for real audiences.

In mini-lessons, teachers demonstrate not only all aspects of the writing process, but various technologies to support children's increasingly independent composition. By focusing on a single aspect of the writing process each day (for example, brainstorming or revision), teachers help children with disabilities gradually make sense of this complex process. By integrating various writing tools into these mini-lessons, teachers help children understand not only how each tool works, but why it is particularly useful. After the mini-lesson, when teachers and aides help children apply the tool and strategy in their own writing, they increase the children's ability to write successfully and independently.

Teachers do not lower their expectations for children with disabilities. They do provide more direct instruction in processes and strategies that they expect children to employ. Teachers also integrate technologies throughout the writing process to help students write more successfully and share that writing in ways that are accessible to all learners.

The multilevel nature of the Writing Block often makes it an ideal route to reading for many children with disabilities. When teachers allow students topic choice and then provide supports for children who find it difficult to choose, students are more likely to be fully engaged in learning activities. When technologies are woven into the writing process to support greater success and independence, children are more likely to find the experience enjoyable and meaningful. When teachers accept individual differences that impact both the quantity and quality of writing, they enable children to progress at their own pace. Finally, when children begin to accurately represent letter-sound relationships in their writing, they begin finding success in using writing to communicate meaningfully with others. Gaining an understanding of the power of print as a communication tool often contributes significantly to children's success in reading for meaning.

Children with Disabilities: Reading and Writing the Four-Blocks® Way • CD-104235 • © Carson-Dellosa

Writing

Summary of the Writing Block

The purposes of this Block are to develop the skill and will of writing while also providing unique opportunities to improve reading skills. Teachers assist children in gaining fluency in recording and revising their ideas and confidence in communicating the ideas to others. This enables children with disabilities not just to write better, but also to read and communicate more effectively.

Mini-Lesson

The teacher presents a mini-lesson in which she models real writing by using one of the "pencils" in the classroom as she teaches a skill or strategy. The mini-lesson has these elements:

- The mini-lesson focuses on some aspect of the writing process—brainstorming, drafting, revising, editing, or publishing.

- The teacher integrates use of the Word Wall, spelling prediction software, communication symbols, adapted keyboards, and other environmental and technological supports for writing ideas and spelling assistance.

- The teacher models use of an editor's checklist with picture communication symbol support to encourage increasing independence in revision, self-checking, and editing an increasingly conventional written product.

Children Writing and Teacher Conferencing

- Students write daily on topics of their own choosing with varying levels of teacher, assistant, and classmate support depending on their abilities and disabilities and the task at hand.

- Individual revision, editing, and publishing conferences are held with designated students who select one piece from 1–2 weeks' worth of first drafts. Teachers assist children in applying editing checklists to final drafts and do not worry about non-conventions that have not yet been addressed in class, although they record them for possible inclusion in the Word Wall, mini-lessons, or other instructional activities. Teachers help children master technologies that enable them to engage in all aspects of the writing process with increasing success and independence.

Author's Chair

- Students share briefly something they have been writing with small peer groups or with the whole class in Author's Chair.

- Authors seek feedback from classmates and respond to their questions.

- Finished pieces are published in the classroom no matter where else they are shared. Publication takes many forms ranging from paper to multimedia.

- Parents, administrators, and classmates are educated to respond more to the content and less to the form of the children's writing.

Writing

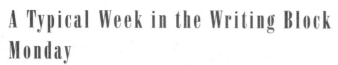

A Typical Week in the Writing Block
Monday

Mini-Lesson: Brainstorming Ideas in Kidspiration®

The teacher suggests that the class brainstorm about grandparents and older people since the class has recently read *Wilfrid Gordon MacDonald Partridge* by Mem Fox (Kane/Miller Book Publishers, 1989). Sitting at a computer linked to a wall-mounted television monitor, the teacher types in Kidspiration® (a software planning tool that integrates pictures and words to support beginning readers and writers) in the main idea bubble: "grandparents and older people." Children call out ideas, "My grandma is called MeMaw," "I went fishing with Grandpa," "My grandma is a good cook," "Old people have gray hair." The teacher types these suggestions on the Kidspiration® screen. As she enters each contribution, she asks, "Does that give anyone a new idea?" After she's entered as many as time permits (or she's exhausted the children's ideas), the teacher works with the students to use the link tool in Kidspiration® to draw an arrow between the main idea and each child's contribution. She also holds the cursor over items in the menu bar so that the children can hear the software speak the item aloud.

Children Writing and Teacher Conferencing

Students begin writing while the teacher conferences with a few of their classmates. After the second conference, with Andrew, she spends a few minutes helping him learn to use Kidspiration® more independently to generate future writing topic ideas. She shows him how and where to save his file, knowing that she will need to review these skills with him in subsequent days.

Author's Chair

Two children take their turns in the Author's Chair. One tells the class before reading, "I'm kind of stuck on how I should end my story. I want to hear what you think after I read." Children praise the story and say they want a happy ending. They like the action and excitement in the story and are concerned that the main character and his dog live happily ever after.

After this discussion, the second child, who has Down syndrome, hesitantly starts to read aloud a knock knock joke. "Knock knock."

"Who's there?" asks the class.

"Blue."

"Blue who?"

"My favorite color is blue."

Other students note that their favorite color is blue. A few mention other favorite colors. One child says, "I bet you could write another good joke about the color you hate most!" Another comments, "I like the part that says, 'blue who?' It makes me think of boo-hoo, like when you're crying." No one seems troubled that the joke lacks a true punch line.

Writing

Tuesday

Mini-Lesson: Copying and Pasting a Kidspiration® Brainstorm into a Word Processor

Today, the teacher opens up the Kidspiration® web that the children generated about their grandparents and older people on Monday. She questions the children briefly about how to type ideas into Kidspiration®, how to hold the cursor over an item to hear it spoken aloud, and how to use the link tool to draw arrows between items. Next, she clicks on the "go to writing" icon, and the class-generated web turns into a sequential outline. She shows the children how to select all of the items, copy them, and paste them into a word processor. Together as a class, they expand on a few ideas within the outline. The two days' mini-lessons are useful to all of the children, but they have been essential for Andrew, who finds it difficult to attend to classroom activities, difficult to sustain concentration in academic tasks, and difficult to organize his thoughts about a topic. Kidspiration® provides him with a tool that sustains its supports through the times when he does attend and enables him to accomplish writing tasks he could not previously do without an adult's assistance.

Children Writing and Teacher Conferencing

The students take out their writing folders to begin writing. Jack, who has significant physical disabilities, sits at the computer with the Intellikeys® keyboard and an alphabet overlay. He types his story in a talking word processor that the aide has opened for him. The aide works hard to remember not to provide too much support. She recalls the teacher helping her understand the difference between supporting Jack to do the best he can do and providing so much support that his product is a better reflection of the best she can do. The teacher holds conferences with a few of the students who are approaching a publication deadline.

Author's Chair

Writing groups of three to four children each meet at tables. Each child takes a turn reading. The first listener then summarizes what was read. The second asks a question about something that is written. The third asks a clarifying question. Each child takes a turn reading and responding in these different ways.

Wednesday

Mini-Lesson: Revision

The teacher projects a transparency with sentences written on it:" I have a grandpa. We call my grandpa "PaPa." My grandpa likes to fish." The teacher reads the sentences aloud and then says, "I wrote this story yesterday after we used Kidspiration to brainstorm. I wonder if you have questions about my grandpa that would help me revise my story."

The children ask questions like, "What kind of fish does your grandpa catch? Where does he live? Do you fish with him? Do you fish in a boat?"

The teacher writes those questions on chart paper for all to see and says, "Those are wonderful questions. Next time I am writing, I will try to imagine what questions you have so that I can write stories that tell you more of what you want to know." She rewrites and thinks

Writing

aloud, recalling some of their questions: I have a grandpa. We call my grandpa "PaPa." My grandpa likes to fish for trout. He lives in the mountains. He doesn't own a boat. He likes to stand in the water when he fishes."

Children Writing and Teacher Conferencing
Students continue working on their writing while the teacher conferences. One student asks the classroom aide to show her how to change the talking word processor from letter and word feedback to word and sentence feedback. She explains that listening to the computer read her story aloud helps her anticipate some of her classmates' responses and questions.

Author's Chair
Three children take turns in the Author's Chair. Each asks the class to listen for something specific before reading. "Which of these two poems do you think I should send to the school newspaper?" says the first. The second sits at the computer with Andrew and says, "Here's my Kidspiration® web of ideas that Andrew and I wrote yesterday. We want to write a story together, and we want to know which ideas sound best to you."

Thursday

Mini-Lesson: Sentence-Combining
The teacher projects the revised text from Wednesday: "I have a grandpa. We call my grandpa 'PaPa.' My grandpa likes to fish for trout. He lives in the mountains. He doesn't own a boat. He likes to stand in the water when he fishes. He wears boots that go up to his waist."

She explains to the class: "One of the things that good writers do is help readers understand how ideas go together. One way they do this is to connect short ideas together in longer sentences. For example, I have two sentences here: We call my grandpa 'Papa.' My grandpa likes to fish for trout." As she writes, she says, "One way I could combine these into a single sentence is to write, 'I have a grandpa called 'Papa,' who likes to fish for trout.' I might also write, 'My grandpa, 'Papa,' likes to fish for trout." The class then works together to combine the final two sentences of the paragraph.

Children Writing and Teacher Conferencing
Students continue writing, some at their desks, some in pairs, some at computers. One student writes on the Smartboard as his work is saved on the computer.

Author's Chair
Writing groups of three to four children each meet at tables. Each group member takes a turn reading, summarizing, questioning, and clarifying.

Children with Disabilities: Reading and Writing the Four-Blocks® Way • CD-104235 • © Carson-Dellosa

Writing

Friday

Mini-Lesson: Multimedia Publication

Today, the teacher takes her text from the previous day and copies and pastes one sentence at a time into PowerPoint® as the children watch. She goes to Google images (*http://www. google.com/imghp?hl=enandtab=wiandq=*) and searches for pictures of fish, people fishing, and fishermen in waders. She copies the images and pastes them into the PowerPoint slides. She asks different children to record their voices reading each slide aloud and adds an action button that readers can click on to hear the words read aloud. She saves the PowerPoint book on the computer desktop library folder. The children already know that they can choose to read electronic books as one of their many options during the Self-Selected Reading Block.

Children Writing and Teacher Conferencing

Students continue writing as the teacher conferences with a few classmates. Today the teacher audio-tapes her interaction with Eric, a boy with autism. She suspects that certain question types are too difficult for him to respond to when she asks him about his writing. She finds later that he successfully responded to all of her what questions, but often said nothing when she asked why he chose certain topics, and simply repeated what she said when she asked him how he came up with certain forms. She has learned from the school's speech-language pathologist (SLP) that how and why questions are the most difficult for children with developmental delays to answer. She will be working with the SLP in coming weeks to structure her interactions not just to better learn what Eric is thinking, but also to help him progress in his understanding of more difficult question forms.

Author's Chair

Two children take turns in the Author's Chair. One, who has significant learning disabilities, and who uses Co:Writer® and WriteOut:Loud® to compose, uses the computer to read his text aloud. He finds it difficult at present to independently read what he composes in this way; he cannot always remember the words the computer spells for him. He asks the class, "What else do you think I should write about race cars in my story?"

Writing

Children with Disabilities: Reading and Writing the Four-Blocks® Way • CD-104235 • © Carson-Dellosa

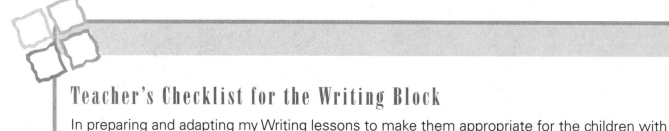

Teacher's Checklist for the Writing Block

In preparing and adapting my Writing lessons to make them appropriate for the children with disabilities in my class, I have:

_____ 1. Selected a single skill or strategy focus in each of my mini-lessons and taught it in a variety of ways so that all my students can learn it.

_____ 2. Varied which of the children's "pencils" I've used as models in each mini-lesson.

_____ 3. Modeled the use of classroom and technological supports for writing, such as Word Wall, talking word processors, spelling prediction software, webbing software, or multimedia publishing.

_____ 4. Modeled each step of the writing process for my students.

_____ 5. Made sure parents or speech-language pathologists have provided needed vocabulary in communication systems of the children with severe communication impairments for peer writing group interactions.

_____ 6. Coordinated with special educators, related services personnel, aides, and parents so that they can support and extend what the children with disabilities are learning this week.

_____ 7. Reduced writing anxiety by using partner and small group writing exercises, provided consistent and positive feedback about relative strengths of a piece of writing, and focused on one to two specific content suggestions for revision.

_____ 8. Motivated composition and attention to convention through the use of real audiences of peers and others within and beyond the classroom.

_____ 9. Published children's writing widely in the classroom, school, and community publications, in multimedia software, and on the Internet.

Children with Disabilities: Reading and Writing the Four-Blocks® Way • CD-104235 • © Carson-Dellosa

Writing

IEP Goals for the Writing Block

Goals for the individualized education plan (IEP) in Writing should reflect the skills and understandings that children are expected to learn as they engage in mini-lessons, writing, and sharing their writing with others. The overall purposes of the Writing Block (page 86) include helping students develop the skills to independently write a wide variety of texts for real purposes on topics of interest, share their writing with peers, and respond to each others' writings. Here are some example goals for Writing arranged from the lowest to the highest skill levels.

1. Given daily opportunities to write about self-selected, personally meaningful topics using the appropriate assistive technologies, the student will independently choose a topic (from his home-school journal, photo journal, or other source) on four out of five days with decreasing levels of prompting.

2. Given daily opportunities to write about self-selected, personally meaningful topics using the appropriate assistive technologies, the student will demonstrate increased complexity as indicated by changes in letter combinations and sequences as well as spaces.

3. Given daily opportunities to write about self-selected, personally meaningful topics using the appropriate assistive technologies, the student will use two- and three-word combinations to express ideas.

4. Given daily opportunities to write about self-selected, personally meaningful topics using the appropriate assistive technologies, the student will link together <insert target number> or more related ideas.

Children with Disabilities: Reading and Writing the Four-Blocks® Way • CD-104235 • © Carson-Dellosa

Writing

in the Working with Words Block, teachers are focused primarily on systematically teaching children the skills they need to read individual words. Teachers guide children in learning how words work and teach them to use words they know to figure out words they don't know. By focusing on use of skills and showing children abstract letter-sound correspondences in real words, teachers help children with disabilities with one of the most difficult aspects of learning to read.

The Word Wall activities provide children with disabilities not only the repetition, but also the variety that is essential to their learning and generalizing of new skills. Each day's different activities encourage children to carefully consider the spelling of each word on the wall. Instead of learning each word to mastery only to struggle to maintain mastery and generalize that knowledge across contexts, children have practice that is distributed over time and promotes long-term learning and retention of the words.

The phonics and decoding activities in the Working with Words Block emphasize both phoneme-by-phoneme and chunking or onset-rime approaches to decoding and spelling. Rules and jargon are avoided in favor of teaching children what to do when they encounter a word that is unfamiliar to them. Teachers direct student learning in these multilevel activities and systematically plan the individual words and skills to be taught.

The Working with Words Block is done knowing that three other Blocks provide rich and varied opportunities to apply the word reading skills children acquire.

Working with Words

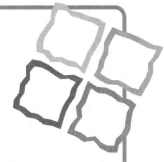

Purposes of the Working with Words Block

The purposes of Working with Words are to:

- help children learn high-frequency words needed for fluent, successful reading with comprehension

- teach children the skills required to decode and spell words they will use for reading and writing

- help children understand how words work

Priorities for Children with Disabilities

Our key consideration, as we make the Working with Words Block accessible to students with a range of disabilities, is maintaining the original purpose of the Block: "children learn to read and spell high-frequency words and the patterns that allow them to decode and spell lots of other words" (Cunningham, Hall, and Defee, 1991). In this chapter, we will describe modifications that allow children with disabilities to participate and learn as part of the general Working with Words Block. While the activities in the Working with Words Block will vary depending on the grade level and time of year, the principles for modification will not. Within each particular activity, remember that there are already children working at a variety of levels. The inclusion of a child with disabilities merely extends that variation. It may take some children with disabilities longer to reach the same goals as peers without disabilities, but the modifications, along with the multilevel nature of the Working with Words Block, increase the likelihood of eventually achieving those goals.

Our priorities when modifying the Working with Words Block for children with disabilities include:

- maintaining the use of letter-by-letter spelling rather than whole word selection or matching

- minimizing the physical demands of letter selection and writing

- differentiating between handwriting and word study

- maintaining a pace of instruction that allows all children to be successful

- establishing a consistent and child-friendly approach to describing letters, words, and spelling patterns

Working with Words

How This Block Matters to Children with Disabilities

For many children with disabilities, the Working with Words Block is a critical component of the Four-Blocks® Literacy Framework. Learning to read words presents a roadblock for students with many different types of disabilities. Some of the roadblocks are the result of specific learning characteristics, and others are the result of the instruction children with disabilities often receive. For example, there are long-standing and erroneous beliefs that children with cognitive impairments can't learn phonics and must only be taught sight-word approaches to reading. Children with other types of disabilities may receive only phonics instruction based on a belief that they must strategically approach each word they encounter to be successful readers. While it is clear that some children find learning sight words easier than phonics and vice versa, without instruction in both, children have a great deal of difficulty learning to read with comprehension.

Working with Words

Word Wall

A successful Word Wall is a vital component of the Four-Blocks® Literacy Framework. The Word Wall is used in activities every day with five new words added to the wall each week. The words are added gradually and practiced repeatedly until they become words that children can read with automaticity, spell with accuracy, and use to read and spell unfamiliar words. Teachers who use a Word Wall successfully make the words on the wall easy for everyone in the classroom to see. They also select the words judiciously, only choosing words that are very common and that children will need often in their reading and writing. They practice the words on the wall every day by clapping, chanting, and writing some of the words. They review the words using a variety of activities. Finally, they systematically support children in using the Word Wall in reading and writing activities throughout the day.

Adaptations: Technologies and Strategies

The day-to-day use of the Word Wall includes four consistent components: providing children with a reason to closely consider as many of the words on the wall as possible, drawing children's attention to particular letters or spelling patterns within words, clapping and chanting the letters of the words, and writing the words. Each of these can present particular challenges for children with disabilities.

Although the teacher makes every effort to make the words on the wall visible to all of the children in the class, some children have a difficult time looking up to the wall and back down at their papers. Other children have visual impairments that make it difficult for them to see the words on the wall. In either case, these children require personal, portable Word Walls.

Teachers in traditional Four-Blocks classrooms often send home updated versions of the Word Wall every week. This practice can be expanded to meet the in-class needs of many children with disabilities. Attaching these weekly updates to a manila folder will allow a child with disabilities to have a Word Wall within easy reach (and sight) at all times. When necessary,

Children with Disabilities: Reading and Writing the Four-Blocks® Way • CD-104235 • © Carson-Dellosa

these portable Word Walls are made more supportive by using a black pen to highlight the shapes of the words and colors that match the classroom Word Wall. Teachers who have successfully created portable Word Walls with color and shape cues have used fluorescent colored paper behind the words on their classroom wall and a highlighter in the same color to mark the words on the portable Word Wall. Rather than inserting a new sheet each week, these teachers use two clear plastic page protectors to cover the sides of the folder and add the five new words each week.

Aa are	**Bb** boy / because	**Cc** car / can't	**Mm**	**Nn** not	**Oo** or / one
Dd don't	**Ee**	**Ff** first	**Pp**	**Qq**	**Rr** rain
Gg girl	**Hh** have	**Ii** I	**Ss** school / saw / said	**Tt** to / two / too / they	**Uu**
Jj	**Kk**	**Ll** little	**Vv**	**Ww** who / was	**XYZ**

There are several advantages to a portable Word Wall for children with disabilities. The addition of color backgrounds helps many children remember the distinction between similar words. The ability to have portable Word Walls on the desks in front of them supports children with visual impairments and other impairments that make it difficult to access the classroom Word Wall. The portable Word Wall also provides a permanent place to add words that are important for the individual child but may not be a part of the classroom Word Wall. On the back of the folder, other words that the child uses often in reading and writing but are not a part of the classroom's Word Wall can be listed. Finally, portable Word Walls can move with children from classroom to classroom, grade level to grade level, and between home and school to provide the repeated practice and application many children will require to successfully learn the words.

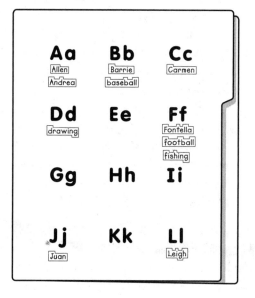

WORKING with WORDS

A portable Word Wall is particularly important for children who use communication systems that are picture based or icon based. Portable Word Walls for these children include symbol and icon supports as needed to help them say the words during lessons, while also learning to spell the words letter by letter. The child who uses the communication device is actively taught to use the symbols for support in saying the whole word when talking about it but to spell the words letter by letter when clapping, chanting, and writing the words.

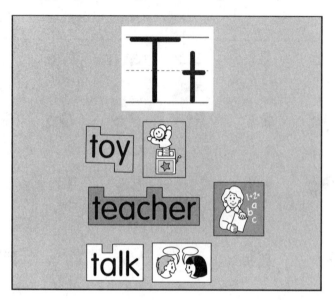

The color cues on the Word Wall serve a special purpose for children with communication impairments who cannot use speech. These children can use a simple color and letter chart to "say" a word on the wall by telling the teacher the letter it begins with and the color behind it (for example, "W—green" might be **what**). This becomes particularly important when a teacher is supporting a child in using the Word Wall to read or spell an unfamiliar word. The teacher can tell the child, "There is a word on the Word Wall that will help you." If the child can't find the word, the teacher can add, "It has a green (or other color) background." If the child still isn't successful in finding the word, the teacher can provide an initial letter clue without actually saying the word, "It begins with a **w**." As a last resort, the teacher can say the word and help the child use the word to read or spell the unfamiliar word, but saying the word, and therefore denying the child to opportunity to learn to develop his own internal phonemic representation of the word, is truly the last resort. Using the clues in this way helps a child gain independence over time in reading and spelling.

One high-tech solution that we recommend using in classrooms where the Word Wall is done well is word prediction software. This type of software provides a list of likely words after each letter is typed. After typing each letter, a student can scan the list looking for the desired word. If the word is in the list, the student can choose it by clicking on the word or typing the number corresponding to it. If the word does not appear after the first letter is typed, a second or perhaps third letter must be typed. At least one prediction program, Co:Writer® (Don Johnston, Inc.), allows the teacher to create and select individualized dictionaries that are used

Children with Disabilities: Reading and Writing the Four-Blocks® Way • CD-104235 • © Carson-Dellosa

Working with Words

for predicting. As words are added to the Word Wall, they can also be added to the prediction dictionary in Co:Writer®, or their frequency rating can be changed in the software to ensure that the word appears early in the prediction cycle.

In addition to the pyramids, people are also fascinated by the sf|

1: **second**
2: **sphinx**
3: **sphinxes**
4: **still**

Word prediction is particularly helpful for children who have motor impairments that make it very difficult for them to keep up with the pace of letter selection required during Working with Words activities in general and the Word Wall in particular. Word prediction will increase a student's rate by decreasing the number of individual letters that must be selected. At the same time, it encourages the student to attend to and produce the spelling of individual words. For Word Wall activities, we do not recommend the use of other rate enhancement techniques that are based on whole-word or phrase selection without spelling.

Children who have high-tech communication devices should always have all of the words on the Word Wall available to them on their devices. However, these words should be incorporated meaningfully into the vocabulary present on the device rather than stored as a separate Word Wall within the device. Many of the high-frequency words that will appear on a primary grades Word Wall will already be a part of the vocabulary in the student's device. Other words will have to be added as they are added to the Word Wall. In either case, as words are added to the wall and introduced, children with communication devices should be shown where the words are available on their devices and how they would use the device to say the words, as well as how to spell them letter by letter.

Teachers who have students with high-tech communication devices in their classes will want to have lists of all of the single-word vocabulary in their students' devices. These vocabulary lists can help the teacher make decisions about which words to add to the Word Wall. For example, a teacher who has identified seven possible words to add to the wall in a given week may decide which five to add by checking the vocabulary to which their students already have access.

The suggestion to include picture and icon supports on portable Word Walls is specific to children who have high-tech communication devices. In general, it is not good practice to pair pictures with words when the goal is word identification. Research suggests that pairing words with pictures slows down the process of learning to read the word, perhaps by distracting attention from the individual letters to the picture. Furthermore, many of the words that beginning readers and writers must learn are not easy to picture. In general, if the goal is teaching the student to read and spell the word, do not pair the word with a picture.

Working with Words

On-the-Back Word Wall Activities

In a typical classroom, it isn't long before children can identify, clap, chant, and write five words in five minutes or less. When this happens, teachers begin completing on-the-back activities after the five words have been completed. The on-the-back activities encourage children to extend what they are learning about the words on the Word Wall.

If there are a few children who are struggling to keep up with the faster pace of the lesson, an on-the-back activity can be planned in such a way that the slower children are focusing on the Word Wall words while the rest of the class is working on the extension skill being taught. For example, a typical on-the-back activity requires children to add word endings to words on the wall. The teacher might read a sentence aloud that includes a Word Wall word with an ending on it. The children listen for the Word Wall word, determine which ending has been added, and then try to write the word with the ending. When there are a few children who are working at a slower pace than the rest of the class, the entire class can use the on-the-back activity time as another opportunity to clap, chant, and write the Word Wall words. This will ensure that everyone claps, chants, and writes each of the five words at least once each (the slower children might complete three in the first part of the lesson and the other two during these on-the-back activities). The rest of the class will then add the appropriate ending.

The Word Wall is a central component of the Working with Words Block. Whatever adaptations are implemented to make it more accessible and successful for children with disabilities, make sure that they do not interfere with the central purpose of the Word Wall: teaching children to read and spell words, including those that are useful in reading and spelling other words.

An Example of Word Wall Adaptation in Action

Ms. Miller claps and counts to five to get the attention of her class, and the children join in as she claps five more times counting down to one. As usual, they all stand quietly to listen for directions after the last clap. Ms. Miller asks them to put away their materials and return to their seats for Word Wall. The children move quickly, each grabbing a pencil and sheet of paper from the bin in the center of the table as they sit down. Linda goes directly to the computer and double-clicks on the word processing program to launch it. Alyssa's assistant puts her lap tray on her wheelchair and gets the color-coded alphabet display mounted on Alyssa's eye-gaze frame. James realizes that everyone is quiet and moves quickly to his seat from the pencil sharpener where he has just finished sharpening his pencil for the third time this morning.

Today, Ms. Miller plans to continue with three of the week's new words that seem to be difficult for the class, and she is going to revisit two words that were added to the wall earlier in the year. She selected these two words because she has noticed that several children in the class are struggling to use them when reading and writing other words even though they have a useful spelling pattern.

Ms. Miller calls out the five words, uses them in sentences, and the children clap, chant, silently chant, and write each word. Linda has her portable Word Wall open next to the computer. It is color-coded just like the class Word Wall, and Alyssa literally touches each word

Children with Disabilities: Reading and Writing the Four-Blocks® Way • CD-104235 • © Carson-Dellosa

Working with Words

that the teacher calls out. Linda is rather enthusiastic in her clapping and cheering. She is a bit slower than her peers in writing the word, but the automatic numbering feature on the word processing program saves her a step and enables her to keep pace.

James is in his seat with his Word Wall open next to his paper. He, too, touches the word on the wall as he successfully identifies it. Ms. Miller stands next to him during the clapping and chanting to allow her physical presence to remind him not to get too loud and carried away. She stays by his side long enough to see him start writing the first letter and moves to check on Alyssa.

The teaching assistant is sitting in front of Alyssa, who has just finished selecting the first letter of the Word Wall. Ms. Miller comments to Alyssa, "Wow! You must have looked really clearly at the group of letters and then the color of the letter you wanted. You selected that letter quickly." Ms. Miller isn't concerned that the letter Alyssa selected is not the correct one because Alyssa is still learning how to use the eye-gaze frame to spell. Ms. Miller observes as Alyssa's assistant points to and names the first letter of the Word Wall word on Alyssa's portable Word Wall. Then, she points to and names the letter Alyssa selected. She asks Alyssa, "**B** and **N**. Are they the same?" Alyssa looks down and to the right to indicate, "No." The assistant continues, "You're right Alyssa. **B** and **N** are not the same. **B** starts the words **best** and **big** on our Word Wall. The letter **N** starts the word **new**. If **new** started with the letter **B**, it would be **bew**." Alyssa chuckles as Ms. Miller walks away to call out the next word.

After the daily Word Wall activities, children move on to 20–25 minutes of Working with Words in the areas of phonics and spelling.

Phonics and Spelling

There are five activities that are used most often in teaching children how to decode and spell new words in the Working with Words Block: Rounding Up the Rhymes, Making Words, Guess the Covered Word, Using Words You Know, and Reading/Writing Rhymes (Cunningham, Hall, and Sigmon, 1999). One of these five activities (or another activity designed by the teacher) is used every day and requires about 20 minutes to complete. Adaptations for the five are discussed here.

Rounding Up the Rhymes

In Rounding Up the Rhymes, the teacher uses a book from a Guided Reading lesson or teacher read-aloud that contains many rhyming words. She selects a section of the book that contains many words that rhyme and share a spelling pattern. While she reads, she encourages the children to chime in whenever they hear any words that rhyme. After reading the book, the children identify the rhyming words again, and the teacher writes them on index cards and puts them in a pocket chart in rhyming pairs. She reminds children that rhyming words usually have the same spelling pattern and invites some children to come and underline the spelling patterns in the pairs and decide whether they are the same or different. The teacher discards any pairs that do not share a spelling pattern and reviews the remaining pairs. Finally, the teacher leads children in a transfer lesson. She writes other words that share spelling patterns with the pairs

Working with Words

in the pocket chart and asks the children to put them with the correct pairs. Once the new words have been placed, the children pronounce the sets of rhyming words, and the teacher says a few other words that the children spell with the help of the spelling patterns on the chart.

Adaptations: Technologies and Strategies

Children with special needs often have a difficult time hearing rhymes or understanding the task involved in detecting rhyming pairs. Some children might benefit from a warm-up activity that gets their ears tuned to listening for rhymes. The teacher or classroom assistant writes two or three of the rhyming words from the text on the board and works with the children to generate a list of rhyming words. Then, the teacher introduces the lesson to the class, reminding the struggling students that they should listen for words that rhyme like those they added to the list.

Other children may require more support. One possibility is to give them word cards with one word from a rhyming pair that exists in the text. As the cards are handed out, the words are read with the children. Children are told to listen for the word in the text and the word that rhymes with it or has the same ending. Some children will only be able to listen for and recognize the word on their card. As they grow successful at this level, they'll be able to move on to listening for the rhyming word that matches the word on their card.

Big books and charts that allow children to see the words that appear in the text can support children with hearing impairments, auditory processing impairments, and other special needs that make it difficult to hear rhymes in words. The visual support can allow them to go from seeing the similar spelling patterns to hearing the rhymes that they produce. While many people assert that hearing rhymes is a precursor to recognizing words in print, there are some children who develop the ability to understand and hear rhyme only after they have learned to recognize and spell some words.

Rounding Up the Rhymes Adaptation in Action

All of the children gather around Ms. Miller on the classroom rug. James sits immediately in his rocking chair. As Linda sits among a group of girls on the rug, Ms. Miller reminds her to get her carpet square so that she can remember to stay in her own space. Alyssa sits on the side with a few other children seated around her in chairs pulled over from the tables. Ms. Miller writes the word **night** on chart paper. She reminds children not to call out as she asks, "Who can tell me something about this word?"

She gives all of the children a few seconds to think before calling on one who says, "It is a Word Wall word!" Another child adds, "It starts with **N**."

Then, Ms. Miller says, "You're right! It is a Word Wall word that starts with **N**. It also has a spelling pattern than can help us read and spell other words. Let's all read the word together. Ready? **Night**. Now, let's do a silent clap and chant for **night**. Ready?" All of the children make clapping motions silently and silently repeat each letter and the whole word.

Ms. Miller continues, "Let's work as a group to figure out as many words as we can that rhyme with the word **night**. Who can get us started?" Ms. Miller writes down every word the children

Children with Disabilities: Reading and Writing the Four-Blocks® Way • CD-104235 • © Carson-Dellosa

Working with Words

suggest, adding those that rhyme under the word **night** and those that do not into a column labeled "Other Words." When children run out of ideas, Ms. Miller asks Alyssa, "Can you choose a letter for us, and we'll see if we can use it to make a rhyming word?" Alyssa works with her assistant and points to the letter B. Ms. Miller asks the class to think about what word they would get if they took away the **N** and replaced it with a **B**. Ms. Miller writes the word **bite** and points out to the children that it rhymes but has a different spelling pattern.

Having spent five minutes on this warm-up, Ms. Miller is confident that Linda, James, and some of her other struggling students will be more successful with the Rounding Up the Rhymes lesson she has planned. She pulls out the Dr. Seuss book they have been reading, *One Fish, Two Fish, Red Fish, Blue Fish* (Random House, 1960). She turns to the page she has marked with a sticky note and tells children she is going to read part of the book and wants them to listen for any words that rhyme like the word **night** did with all of the words on their list. She encourages the children to read along with her and tells them to stop her any time they hear her read words that rhyme.

The assistant puts a BIGmack® communication device on Alyssa's tray and whispers to her, "Alyssa, when you hear rhyming words, you can use your BIGmack® to tell Ms. Miller." Ms. Miller begins reading and barely finishes the first sentence when Alyssa touches the BIGmack®, and it says, "I hear a rhyming pair." Ms. Miller stops and says, "Alyssa says she hears words that rhyme. Has anyone heard any words that rhyme yet?" When no one responds with a yes, Ms. Miller says, "One of the words in this sentence is going to be part of a rhyming pair. Listen while I read the next sentence to see if you can tell me which word it is." She pauses as she finishes the next sentence, many hands shoot up in the air, and again Alyssa uses the BIGmack® to say, "I hear a rhyming pair." Ms. Miller acknowledges Alyssa by saying, "You're right, Alyssa. There is a rhyming pair. Who can tell me what rhyming words you just heard?" Ms. Miller continues the lesson writing the words children hear on index cards and handing them to James to put in the pocket chart two at a time. Occasionally she has to slightly rearrange the words, but this little bit of activity keeps James attentive throughout the lesson.

Making Words

Making Words (Cunningham and Hall, 1994, 1997) is an activity designed to teach children to look for spelling patterns in words and recognize the differences that result when a single letter is changed. Teachers guide children in manipulating their individual set of six to eight letters to create words. The six to eight letters can be arranged to form a "secret" word, but the teacher begins by guiding children through the creation of one-, two-, and three-letter words, and so on, through six- or eight-letter words from the set. The order is carefully selected to help children identify common spelling patterns and recognize the impact of changing one or two letters or the order of a set of letters.

As the children make the words, one child goes to the front of the room and uses a set of large letter cards to make the word for all to use for self-correction. He also puts an index card with the word written on it in a pocket chart before quickly returning to his seat to make the next word. After all of the words have been made, the teacher guides the children in sort and transfer activities that help them focus on the spelling patterns in the words they have made.

Children with Disabilities: Reading and Writing the Four-Blocks® Way • CD-104235 • © Carson-Dellosa

Working with Words

In the sorting activities, the teacher begins by asking children to read all of the words that are in the pocket chart. She then asks the children to group the words that rhyme and share a spelling pattern. She also asks children if they can sort the words based on any other similarities. Sometimes they sort the words for other features (for example, first or last letter, common vowel, length, meaning, or presence of a capital letter).

In the transfer step of the Making Words activity, the teacher writes other words on index cards. She does not just ask children to read the words. Instead, she asks them to tell her which of the words they made would help them read the new word if they encountered it in text. Only after they have identified the correct spelling pattern and put the new word on the chart do they read the new word.

Adaptations: Technologies and Strategies

Making Words lessons can be adapted in ways that do and do not involve computer technology. The light-tech strategies most often involve different types of letter sets that support children who have poor fine motor or impulse control. A sampling of different letter sets includes:

- magnetic letters and a cookie sheet

- a felt board and cards with velcro on them

- a clear acrylic eye-gaze frame with sticky notes or letter cards with self-stick note tape on them

Another simple adaptation that can support children during Making Words is to provide a model of the correct spelling on a child's desk (to self-correct after the initial attempt, not to copy) instead of on the board in the front of the room.

Working with Words

Children with Disabilities: Reading and Writing the Four-Blocks® Way • CD-104235 • © Carson-Dellosa

Children who use picture-based, high-tech communication systems may require a list of the picture symbols or icon sequences so that they can "say" each word efficiently when talking about the words during the sorting and transfer activities.

There are several ways that computers can be used during Making Words to support children with significant motor or attention issues. If the child is able to use a standard keyboard, place the keyboard itself on a copy machine and make a copy. White out all of the letters and make another copy to create a blank template for the keyboard. Leave enough blank paper on the ends to fold around the sides of the keyboard. For every Making Words lesson, punch out the letters that the child will need as well as the delete key, the shift key, and the return key. Use double-sided tape to secure the flaps around the sides of the keyboard itself. These templates can be laminated and stored in the same envelopes as the Making Words lessons themselves.

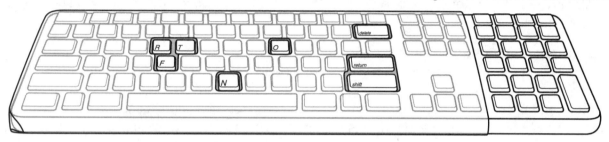

Students who use an alternative keyboard (for example, IntelliKeys® by IntelliTools, Inc.) with the computer can use it for Making Words lessons. An eight-letter template can be created and quickly adapted for most Making Words lessons. Using the appropriate software (for example, Overlay Maker® by IntelliTools, Inc.), create an overlay for the keyboard with spaces for eight letters, shift, delete, and return/enter. Leave the letter spaces blank, print the overlay, and laminate it. Before each lesson, letters can be handwritten into the squares using a grease pencil or write-on/wipe-away marker, leaving spaces blank when lessons require fewer than eight letters. The template is then opened in the software, the appropriate letters are added to the blanks, a save-as command is completed, and the student is ready to go.

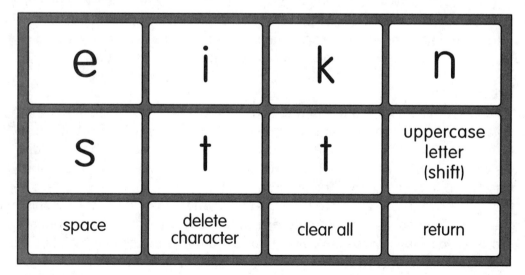

W o r k i n g w i t h W o r d s

Guess the Covered Word

Guess the Covered Word is an activity designed to teach children how to cross-check letter-sound-based decoding strategies with meaning. The teacher writes a sentence on the board covering one word in the sentence with two sticky notes. One note covers the letters preceding the first vowel (the onset) and the other note covers the rest of the word (the rime). The teacher reads the sentence to the class, skipping the covered word, and asks the students to suggest words that would make sense in the sentence. The children provide guesses as the teacher writes them on the board. Then, the teacher removes the first sticky note to reveal the onset. The teacher then leads the children in checking each of their guesses to see which would still be possible given the onset that has been revealed. The children provide additional guesses starting with the revealed onset. When all of the words that fit both the meaning of the sentence and the letters have been guessed, the teacher removes the remaining sticky note to reveal the word.

Adaptations: Technologies and Strategies

This is an important strategy for children with special needs, who have a difficult time cross-checking for meaning once they have decoded a word. These children often read a word incorrectly and keep going because they are not monitoring for meaning. Guess the Covered Word will help them learn how and why it is important to cross-check for meaning while reading.

Guess the Covered Word is one instructional activity tailor-made for children with high-tech communication devices. This activity encourages them to explore the vocabulary on their devices and use vocabulary they may not otherwise use. In this activity and others, teachers model the use of the device to provide appropriate words for the blanks. While thinking aloud, the teacher navigates through the device and finds a word or two that make sense in the sentence.

Children with language impairments may find it difficult to deal with guessing the covered word in complex sentences or sentences with an unusual structure. When beginning to use this strategy with children with language impairments, it may be necessary to use only simple sentences. It may also be necessary to provide examples of words that fit into the blank as well as words that do not fit. Some children might benefit from a bank of these words from which to choose as they are beginning to learn the cross-checking strategy.

Using Words You Know

The goal of this activity is to teach children to use the words they can read and spell to figure out unfamiliar words that share similar spelling patterns. The activity begins with three known words written at the tops of columns. The teacher reviews the words with the children and makes sure each child can read them. Then, the teacher shows children words that rhyme with the word at the top of each column. The children write the words in the appropriate columns and use the known words to help them read the unknown words. All children should have each word written in the appropriate column before anyone is allowed to read the word aloud. After you have completed several words in this way, say a word that rhymes with one of the column

Children with Disabilities: Reading and Writing the Four-Blocks® Way • CD-104235 • © Carson-Dellosa

Working with Words

headers. Ask students to write the word in the appropriate column using the known word to help them spell the unknown word. Throughout these activities, students should be encouraged to explain the strategy they use.

Adaptations: Technologies and Strategies

Children who experience physical impairments or other disabilities that impede their ability to write will require supports to keep up with the pace of these lessons. An example of a light-tech support strategy would be to provide children with their own sets of index cards with the words for the first portion of the lesson written on them. The words to be written at the top of each column are printed on large sticky notes and placed across the top of the student's desk. As the teacher shows the class the word, the child finds the word already printed on an index card, which he then places in the appropriate column on his desk. When it is time to write words, the child can use a set of letter stamps, point to the letters on a laminated alphabet board, or engage in letter-by-letter spelling in ways that reduce the physical demands of handwriting. When a child cannot keep up with the pace of the lesson, even with modifications, it may be more practical for the child to write the onset and point to the appropriate spelling pattern to complete the word.

Alternative keyboards with custom overlays provide high-tech alternatives for Using Words You Know activities. For example, an overlay could be made using a program such as OverlayMaker® (IntelliTools, Inc.) for use with an IntelliKeys® alternative keyboard (IntelliTools, Inc.). The overlay would include the column-header words, the letters of the alphabet, and the spelling patterns in isolation. The child could indicate which column-header word was the correct match by touching it on the keyboard. The child could spell the words shown or spoken by the teacher using a combination of letter-by-letter spelling and the isolated spellings patterns that appear on the overlay.

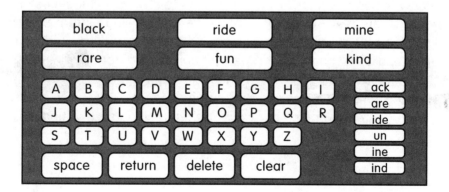

Children with Disabilities: Reading and Writing the Four-Blocks® Way • CD-104235 • © Carson-Dellosa

Working with Words

Reading/Writing Rhymes

In this activity, children learn to use patterns to spell and decode hundreds of words. Children are each given one or two of the 50 onsets (single consonant, blends, digraphs each in a different color) printed on index cards. The teacher writes a rime (single syllable word ending that begins with the first vowel) on a large chart eight times. Children volunteer to come up and make words with the onsets they've been given and the rime on the chart. The teacher records all of the words that can be made and prompts children who have overlooked possible words to come up, saying, "The person who has the **br-** can make a word with this spelling pattern." Later in the year, the teacher will introduce spelling patterns that sound the same but aren't spelled the same.

As the words are made, the teacher works with the children to pronounce the words and decide if they are real words. If the words are real words and spelled correctly, the teacher uses them in sentences and writes them on the chart. If the words are real words that rhyme but have a different spelling pattern, the teacher explains that they are rhyming words with a different spelling and writes them on the bottom of the chart with an asterisk next to each. After all of the words have been made, the teacher encourages children to think of other words they know that rhyme with the collected lists. She records them on the chart as well.

The next step is to work as a group to use the words to write a silly rhyme using lots of the words made by the class. Finally, children are encouraged to write their own rhymes, working with partners as appropriate. The class and individual rhymes are often compiled into a book for the whole class to enjoy.

Adaptations: Technologies and Strategies

Routinely, teachers pay attention to the word reading capabilities of the children in their class when they are passing out the onset cards to the students. Children who are still working on single consonant onsets get those cards, while the most advanced children receive the most difficult and infrequent onsets like **spr-** and **ph-**. Another way in which teachers can encourage the successful participation of children who struggle is to always include a column for "other words." The words that are real words but have a different spelling pattern can be recorded in a column, and all other words children attempt to make are recorded in a third column. Recording words in this "other" column serves two important purposes. First, it ensures that all attempts children make are recorded and treated with the same level of attention and respect. Second, it provides a record of nonexamples to which children can refer when they are trying to use rhymes to help them figure out unfamiliar words in their reading and writing.

Children with Disabilities: Reading and Writing the Four-Blocks® Way • CD-104235 • © Carson-Dellosa

When it comes times to write using the rhyming words, teachers can provide frames that some children might use to complete their silly rhymes. For example:

(Zack) said to (Jack), "Get (back) to the (shack)."

(Mack) sat on a (tack) before eating his (snack).

He put his (pack) on the (rack) and then went out (back).

Developing a Whole-Class Approach That Supports Children with Significant Communication Impairments

Many of the strategies described above involve teaching children the most common spelling patterns to support them in using words they know to read and write words they don't know. Teachers have many different ways that they make decisions regarding which of the many words that share a spelling pattern they will use for the key word they add to the Word Wall. We have found that teachers of children with significant communication impairments should use the child's communication needs as a starting place when determining these words. We begin by generating a list of all of the spelling patterns the teacher plans to teach across the school year. We provide a copy of that list to the child's family and other members of the educational team. They each work to identify words that are meaningful to the child and that represent each spelling pattern. These words might be words that already appear on the child's communication device, or they might be words that should be added to the device to enhance the child's successful face-to-face communication. Once the set of words has been collected, the teacher can then refer to that list when selecting the representative word for the class. The process ensures that the student with communication impairments will have the ability to talk about the key word when using it to read and spell other words, and it won't dramatically change the experience for all of the children in the class.

Making the Working with Words Block Multilevel

Consider a classroom in which there is a child with disabilities much more severe than those experienced by Linda, James, or Alyssa. This child has a very difficult time staying involved in tasks for more than few minutes. He is believed to have severe to profound mental retardation, and he has no formal means of communication. He uses a wheelchair and is dependent on others to move his chair and otherwise meet all of his basic needs. Like many other children with significant disabilities, it is very difficult to determine how much he understands, and there is uncertainty about his vision, hearing, and development in areas such as language. We believe, however, that he, and other children like him, can actively learn and experience success in the general education classroom. The following are examples of his participation in sample Working with Words activities.

Children with Disabilities: Reading and Writing the Four-Blocks® Way • CD-104235 • © Carson-Dellosa

Working with Words

During the Word Wall lessons, he uses a Step-by-Step® (AbleNet, Inc.), a device that can be programmed with several messages in sequence. Programming a message on the Step-by-Step® is as easy as holding down a button, talking, and releasing the button. Each message is then replayed in sequence any time the button is pushed. In the mornings, the teacher, Ms. Miller, programs it so that the child can use it to participate in the clapping and chanting of the words the teacher plans to call that day. Since Ms. Miller knows the order of the words she'll use, she can program the Step-by-Step® to allow the child to call out the words and participate actively.

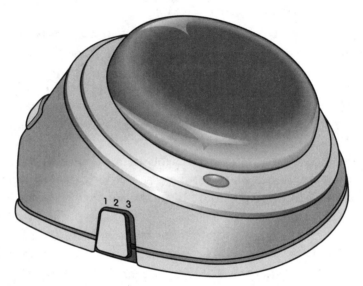

One of the class's favorite Word Wall activities is WORDO. Played like bingo, the children begin by writing nine words from the Word Wall in a 3" x 3" (7.62 cm x 7.62 cm) grid the teacher provides. In most classes, the students take turns picking words from the wall that will be included in the grid. This year Ms. Miller has modified the lesson slightly. The child with significant disabilities has a template on his All-Turn-It Spinner® (AbleNet, Inc.). The All-Turn-It® looks like a wall clock with one hand and no numbers. Words, numbers, and pictures can be added to the clock face, and the clock face can be changed quite easily.

Each week, Ms. Miller adds the new Word Wall words to the Word Wall template that fits on the All-Turn-It® clock face. The child uses a remote switch to make the hand spin. When the

remote switch is released, the clock hand slows to a stop and points at one of the items that was added to the template. On WORDO days, the child selects the nine words by spinning the All-Turn-It® fitted with the Word Wall template. As the children are writing the nine words, the teacher is using a grease pencil to write the nine words on the laminated WORDO template they've created for the All-Turn-It®. Then, the child can use the All-Turn-It® to select the words for the WORDO game.

Children with Disabilities: Reading and Writing the Four-Blocks® Way • CD-104235 • © Carson-Dellosa

Working with Words

A Typical Week in the Working with Words Block
Monday

Word Wall

The teacher begins today's Word Wall lesson by introducing the five new words she has placed on the tray of the board. Because she has students who require more repetition than children she has had in the past, she has included an additional opportunity to focus on each word the first day it is introduced. To so do, she begins by reading each word as she walks around the room and helps the three children with portable Word Walls point to the new words that have been added since last week. Once she is sure each of the children can find the five new words, she repeats each word, uses it in a sentence, and asks the students to clap, chant, and spell each of the words letter by letter. Next, she places the words onto the Word Wall one at a time. As each word is placed on the wall, she once again reads the word, uses it in a sentence, and asks the students to clap, chant, and spell each. Finally, the children write each of the words.

Making Words

This year, the teacher has gotten into the habit of doing Making Words lessons three days each week. In the past she has only done Making Words twice each week. She has based this decision on the needs of the students in her class. Making Words is well-suited to meet the extremely diverse needs of the students in her class (one student is still learning the letters and their associated sounds while several other students read three levels above grade level), and it is one way she can support the special education teacher who is using *Systematic Sequential Phonics They Use* (Cunningham, 2000) with three of the students in her class. The three children receive resource room reading support two mornings each week before the morning bell. On these two mornings, the special education teacher completes a full lesson from *Systematic Sequential Phonics They Use*. On the remaining three days, the children get a complete lesson from *Systematic Sequential Phonics They Use* during their general education class instruction. The children in the general education class are making good progress completing three of every five lessons from *Systematic Sequential Phonics They Use*, and the teacher has not had to give up the other Working with Words activities she has found to be so valuable through the years.

Children with Disabilities: Reading and Writing the Four-Blocks® Way • CD-104235 • © Carson-Dellosa

Working with Words

Tuesday

Word Wall

Today the teacher will use each of the five new words that were added yesterday in sentences she dictates using Word Wall words. The children will first identify the new word in each sentence to clap and chant and write. Then, they will write the entire sentence. Making sentences in this way provides an important level of differentiation that allows her struggling students to focus on clapping, chanting, and writing the target Word Wall words while the other students move on to write the entire sentence.

Guess the Covered Word

The teacher transitions from the Word Wall to the next segment of Working with Words by asking children to gather around her at the easel. As the children move to the carpet, she flips to the chart she has prepared for the Guess the Covered Word activity, and grabs two write-on/wipe-away markers to hand to two students who will record responses on the board. With the exception of the covered word, the sentences the teacher has prepared are comprised largely of words from the Word Wall. Taking care to use these words increases the instructional value of the activity for her struggling readers who get the additional practice they need reading those words in sentences while she addresses their decoding skills.

Wednesday

Word Wall

The words the teacher has chosen to include in her Be a Mind Reader lesson today include three of the new words that appear to be posing the greatest challenge to her students and two words that were posted previously. As the teacher begins, she reads the first clue. The clues she has prepared focus on the meanings of words. She began paying more attention to the purpose of each clue after watching the speech-language pathologist teach a lesson one day. She noticed that the meaning-based clues the speech-language pathologist prepared really extended her students' understandings of the words and got them to think in the same ways she tried to promote through cross checking activities. She still had clues that focused on the orthographic features of the word, but they are far outnumbered by clues that are meaning based.

Making Words

During Making Words today, the teacher tries using a rolling pocket chart stand instead of the board tray to display the letters and words. She has noticed that she purposefully avoids calling on some students to go to the board to make the word for the class using the big letters because it takes them too long or they get so wound up that it is challenging to get them re-engaged in the lesson. Today, she is trying to move the rolling chart stand to the students instead of asking the students to move. Since the students who struggle the most tend to be seated in easy-to-access places where she can regularly circle by and check them, the rolling stand is manageable. While it is more difficult than the tried and true tray in the front of the room, she is the only one who finds it more difficult, and those difficult-to-include children are successfully included.

Children with Disabilities: Reading and Writing the Four-Blocks® Way • CD-104235 • © Carson-Dellosa

Working with Words

Thursday

Word Wall

As the students review endings today, they will use three of the new words that were added to the wall this week (only one is repeated from yesterday) and two words that had been added to the wall previously. To accommodate the pace of the students who struggle the most, she breaks down the activity into two steps. First, the children identify the Word Wall word that is the base of the word she calls out. Once they have identified the word, they clap, chant, and write that word. While the students who struggle the most focus on writing the word, the teacher repeats the word with the ending and asks the students to write the word with its ending. Several of the students who struggle the most do not have time to write the word with the ending before they move on to the next word, but they all have a chance to clap, chant, and write the base Word Wall word.

Using Words You Know

Today, the teacher has decided to do a student-directed three-column sort to help children learn to use the words they know to read and spell other words. She begins by selecting three words from the Word Wall that have spelling patterns that are helpful in reading and spelling other words. The lesson begins with the teacher calling out those words for the children to write as the headers of the three columns on the paper she has given them. As the students write the words on their papers, the teacher writes them on the top of columns she has drawn on the board. She adds one more column with the header "Other" to the board.

Next, she asks the students to help her think of words that both rhyme and share a spelling pattern with one of the words they've written. As the children call out words, she asks the group to point to the right (the windows), the left (the door), or up (the ceiling) to show if they think the word goes in right, left, or center column. She uses this type of every pupil response as often as possible because it allows her to provide enough time for all of the children to process since she has all of the students respond on the count of three. Once she's had a chance to see how each of the students has responded, she can then call on one who has indicated a correct response.

Children with Disabilities: Reading and Writing the Four-Blocks® Way • CD-104235 • © Carson-Dellosa

Friday

Word Wall

For today's cross-checking lesson, the teacher begins by calling out five words that all begin with the same letter. The children clap, chant, and write each of the five words. Then, the teacher asks the students to read sentences she has written on the board with one word omitted from each. The students have to decide which of the five words they've written would complete each sentence. As with Guess the Covered Word, the teacher has used Word Wall words as much as possible in writing the sentences so that all of the children can be successful in reading the sentences with her. The fact that the children are successful in reading most of the words allows them to focus their attention on the meaning of the sentence and the word that best fits in the blank. This will prepare them more directly for applying the skill as needed when reading connected text and encountering an unfamiliar word.

Making Words

The teacher completes a third lesson from *Systematic Sequential Phonics They Use* (Cunningham, 2000).

Children with Disabilities: Reading and Writing the Four-Blocks® Way • CD-104235 • © Carson-Dellosa

Working with Words

Children with Disabilities: Reading and Writing the Four-Blocks® Way • CD-104235 • © Carson-Dellosa

Teacher's Checklist for the Working with Words Block

In preparing and adapting my Working with Words lessons to make them appropriate for the children with disabilities in my class, I have . . .

_____ 1. Added words I've selected for the Word Wall to the communication devices my children with communication impairments use.

_____ 2. Ensured that all children will have the time required to spell the words letter by letter rather than selecting them as whole words.

_____ 3. Used technologies and modifications as necessary to decrease the physical demands of selecting or writing letters.

_____ 4. Created a portable Word Wall with appropriate supports for each child.

IEP Goals for the Working with Words Block

Goals for the individualized education plan (IEP) in Working with Words should reflect the skills and understandings that children are expected to learn as they engage in learning to read and spell words. While the progress in the IEP goals listed below is based on performance during other Blocks, they represent important ways to measure progress in the application of the skills being taught in the Working with Words Block. The very nature of the instruction during the Working with Words Block should allow children to be highly successful during the Working with Words activities. Children's true progress is indicated by how well they apply the skills acquired during the Working with Words Block when they are reading and writing. Here are some example goals for Working with Words arranged from the lowest to the highest skill levels.

1. Given daily opportunities to participate in Word Wall instruction, the student will independently use the Word Wall as a support in reading and writing at least three times each day.

2. Given regular opportunities to engage in first draft writing (i.e., writing without standards), the student will accurately spell 8 of 10 high-frequency words he/she chooses to use.

3. Given the opportunity to reread a passage at his/her current reading level, the student will accurately identify 97 percent of the words and maintain a <insert target words per minute rate> words-per-minute rate.

4. Given a passage at <insert level one or more levels higher than current> reading level, the student will successfully decode 97 percent of the single-syllable words that contain high-utility onsets and rimes.

Working with Words

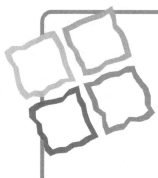

Questions and Answers

As teachers and related services personnel attempt to support the literacy learning needs of students with disabilities, they inevitably run into a variety of interesting instructional challenges. When we talk with educators around the country, we are asked all sorts of important questions about these challenges. We have attempted to answer some of the most commonly asked questions below.

Q: How do I work with the special education teacher to support the children with disabilities in my Four-Blocks classroom?

A: There is no one way that is best, but we do know that working together is important. For years, receiving special education support meant getting out of the general education classroom, and there is no good time to be absent from the classroom. Leaving during any portion of reading and writing instruction results in missed opportunities for instruction that will be referred to across the rest of the day, week, and school year. Leaving during social studies or science results in missed opportunities to develop important background knowledge and potential difficulties with comprehension at a later date. There is just no good time to get pulled out of the general education classroom to receive special education instruction.

In one school where we've worked, the teachers (both general and special education) realized that something wasn't working with their pull-out model. We sat down with them to help them determine what wasn't working and help them find workable alternatives to their long-standing approach. Our discussion and subsequent observations suggested that the children with disabilities did quite well during the two teacher-directed Blocks in the general education classroom: Guided Reading and Working with Words. The students appeared to be struggling to apply what they were learning in these two Blocks during the Writing and Self-Selected Reading Blocks.

Children with Disabilities: Reading and Writing the Four-Blocks® Way • CD-104235 • © Carson-Dellosa

Children with Disabilities: Reading and Writing the Four-Blocks® Way • CD-104235 • © Carson-Dellosa

Q: When is the best time for the speech-language pathologist to work with students in my class?

A: Language is the core of both reading and writing. As such, the speech-language pathologist (SLP) can be particularly supportive during the Guided Reading and Writing Blocks. During Guided Reading, the SLP might work with the whole class or a small group to build background knowledge regarding a new or particularly complex topic. This instruction might include vocabulary instruction that is focused on teaching children the relationships between words (SLPs call these semantic relationships) that help children learn a strategy for linking new words to known words and experiences. The SLP can also provide support during Guided Reading by helping to create after-reading tasks that focus directly on building language comprehension.

During the Writing Block, the SLP can be particularly helpful with students who have a hard time generating and organizing ideas. Many children receiving speech and language services at school find this part of writing particularly difficult. The SLP can work with these children to generate word and idea banks related to a selected topic. Once the words are generated, the SLP can help children visually map the relationships among the words and ideas. The SLP might also work with children to help them improve their sentence structure (syntax) during writing.

Q: The occupational therapist wants to work with her children during the Writing Block because many of their goals are focused on improved handwriting. Is that the best time?

A: It depends! If the children can select a topic, dictate a complete story with ease, and spell the words they choose, then it is probably okay to have the SLP add the focus on handwriting during the Writing Block. However, most children receiving services from an occupational therapist (OT) have difficulties with aspects of writing in addition to handwriting. In this case, adding the focus on the motor demands of handwriting on top of the need to generate ideas, translating those ideas into words and sentences, spelling those words, and composing the actual text is too much. Consider having the OT support

Questions and Answers

the student during the Working with Words Block when some of the language demands are decreased. This is the time when handwriting is often the focus for Four-Blocks classrooms in schools with a handwriting curriculum.

Is there research to support the use of Four-Blocks with children with disabilities?

One published study (Hedrick, Katims, and Carr, 1999) describes the successful implementation of a Four-Blocks program in a special education classroom serving nine elementary school students with mild to moderate mental retardation (mean IQ was 58, range 40–76). The results indicate that a Four-Blocks approach to reading intervention led to improved student achievement across two formal measures of reading ability (Brigance Diagnostic Comprehensive Inventory of Basic Skills [Brigance, 1983] and the Test of Early Reading Ability–2 [TERA–2; Reid, Hresko, and Hammill, 1989]) and five informal measures (Concepts about Print, Story Retellings, Writing, Word Decoding, and the Analytical Reading Inventory [ARI; Woods and Moe, 2002]). The students received balanced literacy instruction for a total of three hours each day across an entire school year with 45 minutes devoted to each of the Four Blocks.

A second published study demonstrates the success of the components of the Four Blocks with one 11-year-old boy with severe cerebral palsy and communication impairments. For example, this boy learned to use spelling as a means of communication as a direct result of daily Making Words instruction (Erickson, Koppenhaver, Yoder, and Nance, 1997). Making Words and Using Words You Know were also instrumental in supporting the successful outcomes of a group of 14–21-year-old students with significant developmental disabilities including communication impairments.

Questions and Answers

Children with Disabilities: Reading and Writing the Four-Blocks® Way • CD-104235 • © Carson-Dellosa

**Q:**

As a classroom teacher, do I include my special education students who haven't learned to identify letters or developed concepts about print in my Four-Blocks instruction?

**A:**

Yes. The challenge is to make your instruction even more multilevel than you would have to without that child in your class. We have found that we can continue to develop concepts about print and language comprehension with our students with the most significant disabilities during the Guided Reading and Self-Selected Reading Blocks. During Guided Reading, these students are more likely to participate in reading with the teacher and a small group of students so that we can be sure they are getting a good shared reading experience. We can point out the features of the book, encourage their maximal participation in making comments, completing predictable lines, and interacting with us while we read with them. During Self-Selected Reading, we can support these students by using computerized books or reading aloud the books they select in a shared rather than independent reading context. While these students may not be able to engage in independent self-selected reading for the same length of time as your other students, it is important that they have the same daily opportunities to independently select and explore books.

Likewise, we have found that the Working with Words and Writing Blocks provide a meaningful way to help children learn letter names and sounds and other important alphabet concepts. During Working with Words, students can learn the letters and their sounds while engaged in the same activities that are teaching other students to read and spell words. For example, in one classroom, a girl who did not know any letter names participated fully in Making Words. She had at least one opportunity to learn the letter names and sounds as the children gathered the letters required for the lesson. She then had dozens of repeat opportunities to hear those letter names and sounds as she made her word look like the model that was created on the chalk tray at the front of the room. It wasn't long before she was able to find the first and then last letters of the words before the model was provided. After years of unsuccessful drills with letter matching and letter identification, Making Words provided a meaningful, motivating context within which she rapidly learned and began applying her knowledge of letter names and sounds.

In a similar way, the Writing Block provides a meaningful context for children who have not developed concepts about print and alphabet concepts to develop those skills. All of the children we work with have the opportunity to write every day,

Questions and Answers

even if they do not know a single letter. We can talk about the letters they type, use a talking word processor to give them feedback while they're composing the text, and use the texts they create (long before we can actually read them) as the basis of our instruction.

Don't confuse our eagerness to include students maximally in multilevel classroom instruction with an endorsement of using the Four Blocks with young children or in special education classrooms where the majority of the students have NOT emerged as readers and writers. When the children who don't know letters and don't have concepts about print represent the majority of your students, consider the Building Blocks as a framework for your classroom literacy instruction. You can learn about the Building Blocks in a video called Building Blocks (Cunningham and Hall, 1996) or read about it in *Month-by-Month Reading, Writing, and Phonics for Kindergarten* (Hall and Cunningham, 1997, 2003). This different approach to organizing the components of the Four Blocks emphasizes reading to, with, and by students; writing for, with, and by students; and many activities that develop knowledge of words, letters, and sounds.

I recently saw software that would let me put a picture, like a rebus symbol, with every word in the materials we use. How can I use that software to support my students with disabilities?

In general, the research does not support the practice of representing every word in a text with a picture/symbol. Nor does it support pairing individual words with pictures/symbols during Working with Words instruction. While it is clear that children do eventually learn the words that are paired with the pictures/symbols, they will learn the words more quickly if the pictures are not there. The reason isn't 100 percent clear, but it appears as though the pictures/symbols linked with individual words actually draw the child's attention away from the print. Learning to read requires careful attention to the words and the letters, so you want to stay away from any practice that distracts children from the letters and words.

This is not to say that there aren't many times when it makes sense to provide children with picture/symbol support when reading. Text that is supported by pictures/symbols will allow some children to independently access information that they otherwise would not be able to read. Pictures/symbols can also help children achieve more independence in following the classroom routine and simple directions.

Children with Disabilities: Reading and Writing the Four-Blocks® Way • CD-104235 • © Carson-Dellosa

Questions and Answers

Children with Disabilities: Reading and Writing the Four-Blocks® Way • CD-104235 • © Carson-Dellosa

One of the students in my class has Down syndrome. I remember from a special education class that I took in college that children with cognitive impairments can't learn phonics. Should this child be included in my Working with Words Block?

Your memory isn't failing you. It used to be widely believed that children with Down syndrome and other forms of cognitive impairments had to learn to read using whole-word approaches. The result was that most of these children never advanced beyond the earliest levels of reading because we all know that readers must have the ability to figure out unfamiliar words if they are going to be successful. Fortunately, the research now supports our understanding of the fact that individuals with Down syndrome can acquire phonological awareness and learn phonics. Furthermore, there is specific research to support the use of the kind of instruction used in the Working with Words Block. For example, one study compared a whole-word and an analytic approach with two groups of children with Down syndrome (Cupples and Iacono, 2002). The analytic approach was very similar to the Word Wall and Using Words You Know strategies taught in the Working with Words Block. The children in both the whole-word and analytic groups learned the words they were taught, but the children in the analytic group also learned to use the words they had been taught to read unfamiliar words that had the same spelling pattern.

Won't using a computer for writing keep my students from learning to write with a pencil?

Not at all! Many children with disabilities, even those without obvious physical disabilities, find it very difficult to learn to write when they have to juggle the demands of handwriting on top of everything else they're learning. Providing them with the opportunity to use the computer or some other form of technology while they learn what it means to be a writer allows them to make more rapid progress. Eventually, they'll be successful enough as writers that learning to write with a pencil will be much easier—and the students will be much more motivated to improve their handwriting because they'll have a better understanding of how important it is for their audiences to read what they've written.

Questions and Answers

Q: The special education teacher has suggested that I use red for all of the vowels when I put words on my Word Wall. She says it will help my students with disabilities learn the vowel patterns and improve their spelling. Will it?

A: It may help them learn vowel patterns, but it defeats one of the primary purposes of the Word Wall: helping children learn to recognize the most frequent spelling patterns that they can use to read and spell hundreds of other words. Highlighting just the vowels in red will take children's attention away from the entire spelling pattern (rime) that you are trying to highlight for all of the children. You might then ask, why not highlight the whole spelling pattern by using red font? Well, that would help children learn those spelling patterns, but their eyes would be drawn away from the spelling of the whole word and focus only on the letters in red. We think the traditional Word Wall practice of underlining spelling patterns that can be used to help read and write other words is the best practice. It provides children with some support in finding those words that are most useful without drawing their attention away from every letter in every word on the Word Wall.

Children with Disabilities: Reading and Writing the Four-Blocks® Way • CD-104235 • © Carson-Dellosa

Questions and Answers

Professional References Cited

- Brigance, A. H. 1983. *Brigance diagnostic comprehensive inventory of basic skills.* North Billerica, MA: Curriculum Associates.

- Cunningham, P. M. 1979. Beginning reading without readiness: Structured language experience. *Reading Horizons* 19 (3): 222–227.

- Cunningham, P. M. 2000. *Systematic sequential phonics they use.* Greensboro, NC: Carson-Dellosa.

- Cunningham, P. M., and D. P. Hall. 1994. *Making words: Multilevel, hands-on, developmentally appropriate spelling and phonics activities.* Parsippany, NJ: Good Apple.

- Cunningham, P. M., and D. P. Hall. 1997. *Making more words: Multilevel, hands-on phonics and spelling activities.* Parsippany, NJ: Good Apple.

- Cunningham, P. M., D. P. Hall, and M. Defee. 1991. Non-ability grouped, multilevel instruction: A year in a first-grade classroom. *The Reading Teacher* 44 (8): 566–572.

- Cunningham, P. M., D. P. Hall, and C. M. Sigmon. 1999. *The teacher's guide to the Four Blocks®.* Greensboro, NC: Carson-Dellosa.

- Cupples, L., and T. Iacono. 2002. The efficacy of "whole word" versus "analytic" reading instruction for children with Down syndrome. *Reading and Writing: An Interdisciplinary Journal* 15 (5–6): 549–574.

- Erickson, K. A., D. A. Koppenhaver, D. E. Yoder, and J. Nance. 1997. Integrated communication and literacy instruction for a child with multiple disabilities. *Focus on Autism and Other Developmental Disabilities* 12 (3): 142–150.

- Hall, D. P., and P. M. Cunningham. 1997, 2003. *Month-by-month reading, writing, and phonics for kindergarten.* Greensboro, NC: Carson-Dellosa.

- Hedrick, W. B., D. S. Katims, and N. J. Carr. 1999. Implementing a multimethod, multilevel literacy program for students with mental retardation. *Focus on Autism and Other Developmental Disabilities* 14 (4): 231–239.

- Koch, K. 2000. *Wishes, lies, and dreams: Teaching children to write poetry.* New York: Harper Paperbacks.

- Manzo, A. 1969. The ReQuest procedure. *The Journal of Reading* 13 (2): 123–126.

- McCracken, R. A., and M. J. McCracken. 1986. *Stories, songs, and poetry to teach reading and writing.* Winnipeg: Peguis Publishers.

- Ogle, D. M. 1986. K-W-L: A teaching model that develops active reading of expository text. *The Reading Teacher* 39 (6): 564–570.

Resources

- Palincsar, A. S., and A. L. Brown. Interactive teaching to promote independent learning from text. *The Reading Teacher* 39 (8): 771–777.

- Raphael, T. E., and K. H. Au. 2005. QAR: Enhancing comprehension and test taking across grades and content areas. *The Reading Teacher* 59 (3): 206–221.

- Reid, D. K., W. P. Hresko, and D. D. Hammill. 1989. TERA–2: *Test of early reading ability–2*. Minneapolis, MN: Pearson Assessments.

- Stauffer, R. G. 1969. *Teaching reading as a thinking process*. New York: Harper and Row.

- Woods, M. L., and A. J. Moe. 2002. *Analytical reading inventory* (7th ed.). Upper Saddle River, NJ: Prentice Hall.

Children's Books Cited

- *ABC for You and Me* by Margaret Girnis (Albert Whitman & Company, 2000)

- *Apt. 3* by Ezra Jack Keats (Puffin, 1999)

- *Be Good to Eddie Lee* by Virginia Fleming (Philomel, 1993)

- *Bubba and Trixie* by Lisa Campbell Ernst (Simon and Schuster, 1997)

- The *Captain Underpants* Series by Dav Pilkey (Blue Sky Press/Scholastic)

- *Dad and Me in the Morning* by Patricia Lakin (Concept Books, 1994)

- *Dina the Deaf Dinosaur* by Carol Addabbo (Hannacroix Creek Books, 1998)

- *Fireboat: The Heroic Adventures of the John J. Harvey* by Maira Kalman (Puffin, 2005)

- *Flying Firefighters* by Gary Hines (Clarion Books, 1993)

- *Harry and Willy and Carrothead* by Judith Caseley (Greenwillow, 1991)

- *The Hickory Chair* by Lisa Rowe Fraustino (Arthur A. Levine, 2001)

- *I Have a Sister: My Sister Is Deaf* by Jeanne Whitehouse Peterson (HarperCollins, 1977)

- *Ian's Walk: A Story about Autism* by Laurie Lears (Albert Whitman and Company, 1998)

- *If You Give a Mouse a Cookie* by Laura Joffe Numeroff (Laura Geringer, 1985)

- *Kelly's Creek* by Doris Buchanan Smith (Crowell, 1975)

- *Knots on a Counting Rope* by Bill Martin, Jr., and John Archambault (Henry Holt, 1997)

- *The Lonely Scarecrow* by Tim Preston (Dutton Children's Books, 1999)

Children with Disabilities: Reading and Writing the Four-Blocks® Way • CD-104235 • © Carson-Dellosa

Resources

- *Mama Zooms* by Jane Cowen-Fletcher (Scholastic, 1993)

- *Moses Goes to the Circus* by Isaac Millman (Farrar, Strauss, and Giroux, 2003)

- *Moses Goes to a Concert* by Isaac Millman (Farrar, Strauss, and Giroux, 1998)

- *Moses Goes to School* by Isaac Millman (Farrar, Strauss, and Giroux, 2000)

- *Mouse Paint* by Ellen Stoll Walsh (Harcourt Big Books, 1991)

- *My Buddy* by Audrey Osofsky (Henry Holt, 1992)

- *My Friend Isabelle* by Eliza Woloson (Woodbine House, 2003)

- *My Friend Jacob* by Lucille Clifton (Dutton, 1980)

- *On My Beach There Are Many Pebbles* by Leo Lionni (Mulberry, 1961)

- *One Fish, Two Fish, Red Fish, Blue Fish* by Dr. Seuss (Random House Books for Young Readers, 1960)

- *Otto Is Different* by Franz Brandenberg (Greenwillow, 1985)

- *A Picture Book of Helen Keller* by David Adler (Holiday House, 1992)

- *A Picture Book of Louis Braille* by David Adler (Holiday House, 1997)

- *A Place for Grace* by Jean Davies Okimoto (Sasquatch Books, 1993)

- *Red Riding Hood Races the Big Bad Wolf* by Richard Paul (Twilight Press, 1999)

- *Rolling Along with Goldilocks and the Three Bears* by Cindy Meyers (Woodbine House, 1999)

- *Russ and the Almost Perfect Day* by Janet Rickert (Woodbine House, 2001)

- *Russ and the Apple Tree Surprise* by Janet Rickert (Woodbine House, 1999)

- *Russ and the Firehouse* by Janet Rickert (Woodbine House, 2000)

- *The Secret Code* by Dana Meachen Rau (Children's Press, 1998)

- *Seven Blind Mice* by Ed Young (Philomel, 1992)

- *Silent Lotus* by Jeanne Lee (Sunburst, 1994)

- *Spiders* by Gail Gibbons (Holiday House, 1994)

- *Squids Will Be Squids* by Jon Scieszka and Lane Smith (Viking Juvenile, 1998)

- *The Stranger* by Chris Van Allsburg (Houghton-Mifflin, 1986)

Children with Disabilities: Reading and Writing the Four-Blocks® Way • CD-104235 • © Carson-Dellosa

Resources

- *Susan Laughs* by Jeanne Willis (Henry Holt and Company, 2000)

- *Talking to Angels* by Esther Watson (Harcourt Brace, 1996)

- *Through Grandpa's Eyes* by Patricia MacLachlan (Harper Trophy, 1980)

- *Tough Boris* by Mem Fox (Voyager Books, 1998)

- *Tuesday* by David Wiesner (Clarion Books, 1991)

- *We'll Paint the Octopus Red* by Stephanie Stuve-Bodeen (Woodbine House, 1998)

- *Why Am I Different?* by Norman Simon (Albert Whitman and Company, 1976)

- *Wilfrid Gordon MacDonald Partridge* by Mem Fox (Kane/Miller, 1989)

Children with Disabilities: Reading and Writing the Four-Blocks® Way • CD-104235 • © Carson-Dellosa

Resources

Software and Hardware Manufacturers

- **Ablenet, Inc.**
  800-322-0956 US and Canada
  http://www.ablenetinc.com
  All-Turn-It® Spinner, BIGmack®, Step-by-Step Communicator, BookWorm™

- **AOL Instant Messenger (AIM®)**
  http://www.aim.com/

- **Apple Computer, Inc.**
  http://www.apple.com
  800-MY-APPLE
  AppleWorks, Quicktime 7 (http://www.apple.com/quicktime/download/mac.html)

- **Brøderbund**
  http://www.broderbund.com
  800-395-0277
  KidPix® Studio Deluxe 4

- **Bytes of Learning, Inc.**
  http://www.bytesoflearning.com
  800-465-6428
  MP Express®

- **Don Johnston, Inc.**
  http://www.donjohnston.com
  800-999-4660
  Co:Writer®, Draft:Builder®, Read:OutLoud™, Start-to-Finish® Literacy Starters and Readers, Write:OutLoud®

- **Inspiration, Inc.**
  http://www.inspiration.com
  800-877-4292
  Inspiration®, Kidspiration®

- **Intellitools, Inc.**
  http://www.intellitools.com
  IntelliKeys® USB, IntelliPics, IntelliTalk, Overlay Maker® 3

- **Lego, Inc.**
  http://www.lego.com
  800-422-5346
  Duplo®

Children with Disabilities: Reading and Writing the Four-Blocks® Way • CD-104235 • © Carson-Dellosa

Resources

- **Microsoft Corporation**
  http://www.office.microsoft.com
  800-642-7676
  PowerPoint®, Windows®

- **ReadPlease Corporation**
  http://www.readplease.com
  866-727-8958
  ReadPlease®

- **Riverdeep, Inc.**
  http://www.riverdeep.com
  888-242-6747
  Living Books® Library

- **SMART Technologies**
  http://www.smarttech.com
  888-42-SMART
  SMART Board™

- **SoftTouch, Inc.**
  http://www.softtouch.com
  877-763-8868)
  My Own Bookshelf

- **Sunburst Technology, Inc.**
  http://www.hyperstudio.com
  800-492-8817
  · HyperStudio®

- **Toys for Special Children (Children's Catalog)**
  Enabling Devices
  http://enablingdevices.com
  800-832-8697
  Cheap Talk 4

- **Turning Point Therapy and Technology, Inc.**
  http://www.turningpointtechnology.com
  830-608-9812
  Keyguard

Children with Disabilities: Reading and Writing the Four-Blocks® Way • CD-104235 • © Carson-Dellosa

Resources